WorshipPoints
A Liturgical Resource for Year A

Chris Warren

Parson's Porch Books
www.parsonsporchbooks.com

WorshipPoints: A Liturgical Resource for Year A

ISBN: Softcover 978-1-949888-23-2
Copyright © 2018 by Chris Warren

All rights reserved. No part of this book may be reproduced or transmitted in any form or by any means, electronic or mechanical, including photocopying, recording, or by any information storage and retrieval system, without permission in writing from the publisher.

WorshipPoints

Contents

First Sunday of Advent 9
Second Sunday in Advent 11
Third Sunday of Advent 13
Fourth Sunday of Advent 15
Nativity of the Lord 17
First Sunday After Christmas 19
Second Sunday after Christmas Day 21
Epiphany 23
First Sunday after Epiphany 25
Second Sunday after the Epiphany 27
Third Sunday after the Epiphany 29
Fourth Sunday after the Epiphany 31
Fifth Sunday after the Epiphany 33
Sixth Sunday after the Epiphany 35
Seventh Sunday after the Epiphany 37
Eighth Sunday after the Epiphany 39
Ninth Sunday after the Epiphany 41
Transfiguration Sunday 43
Ash Wednesday 45
First Sunday of Lent 47
Second Sunday of Lent 49
Third Sunday of Lent 51
Fourth Sunday of Lent 53
Fifth Sunday of Lent 55
Liturgy of the Palms 57
Liturgy of the Passion 59
Resurrection of the Lord 61

Resurrection of the Lord Alternate 63
Second Sunday of Easter.. 65
Third Sunday of Easter... 67
Fourth Sunday of Easter... 69
Fifth Sunday of Easter.. 71
Sixth Sunday of Easter... 73
Seventh Sunday of Easter... 75
Ascension of the Lord 77
Day of Pentecost... 79
Trinity Sunday 81
Proper 3 83
Proper 4 85
Proper 5 87
Proper 6 89
Proper 7 91
Proper 8 93
Proper 9 95
Proper 10 97
Proper 11 99
Proper 12 101
Proper 13 103
Proper 14 105
Proper 15 107
Proper 16 109
Proper 17 111
Proper 18 113
Proper 19 115
Proper 20 117

Proper 21 119
Proper 22 121
Proper 23 123
Proper 24 125
Proper 25 127
Proper 26 129
Proper 27 131
Proper 28 133
Proper 29 Reign of Christ 135
All Saints Day... 137

First Sunday of Advent

Scripture
Isaiah 2:1-5
Psalm 122
Romans 13:11-14
Matthew 24:36-44

Call to Worship
One: I was glad when they said to me
Let us go to the house of the LORD.
Many: It is good to be within your gates, Mighty God.
We have come to worship you.
One: May peace reign in all the places where God's name is extolled.
May God's presence fill the entire world.
Many: Let all peoples of the world praise God.
Let the mountain of the LORD be raised up.
One: For the sake of the house of the LORD,
Let us seek the good of God's Temple.
Many: O House of Jacob, come!
Let us walk in the light of the LORD!

Invocation
We are glad to be in your house, Great God of all creation. Open our eyes to see your glory. Open our ears to hear your voice. Open our hearts that we may devote ourselves to you and to your desires for this world. Make this church a beacon to the community and to the world. Let all who come here know they have truly worshiped you.

Call to Confession
Salvation is nearer to us now than when we first believed. We who are God's children have erred and fallen away from the path of salvation God has placed before us. Sinfulness is the human condition. We pray now to God, trusting in God's mercy and willingness to forgive.

Prayer of Confession
God of grace, we have failed to follow your paths for our lives. We have given in to greed, to anger, and to desire. We are a sinful people. Apart from your mercy, we cannot be made whole. Hear us as we pray to you. Forgive the ways we have failed to love you completely and to love one another as ourselves. Help us to set aside those ways and live for you.

Assurance of Forgiveness
It is a gracious and forgiving God we serve. When we turn to God in willingness to repent--to set aside our sins and sin no more-- God is faithful to forgive. God wipes the slate clean, and we are made whole once again. Thanks be to God.

Offertory Invitation
In the days of Noah, many were only concerned with their own comfort and satisfaction. They had forgotten how to care for one another. The moment of offering is an opportunity for the church to show its continuing care for each other and the world. We give that the world may be made more like Christ's coming kingdom.

Offertory Prayer
LORD of all things, we have given this day only a small portion of what you have entrusted to us. We pray that you will find us faithful, and that you will accept our gifts. We ask that you bless them that we might do your work throughout our community and the world. Amen.

Benediction
We have been to the house of God. We have worshiped God here. May the peace of God be on this place, on every place where God is worshiped, and on each one of us, both now and forever more. Amen.

Second Sunday in Advent

Scripture
Isaiah 11:1-10
Psalm 72:1-7, 18-19
Romans 15:4-13
Matthew 3:1-12

Call to Worship
One: The coming king will judge with righteousness.
He will judge the poor with justice.
Many: May the mountains yield prosperity for the people.
May righteousness flow from the hills.
One: He will defend the cause of the poor
He will deliver the needy and crush the oppressor.
Many: He will live and reign throughout all generations.
His mercy will rain like showers that water the earth.
One: In all his days, righteousness will flourish.
Peace will abound until time is no more.
Many: Blessed be the LORD, the God of Israel.
Who alone does wondrous things.
May God's glory fill the whole earth.

Invocation
We bow before you, Great God of the Universe, in thanksgiving for the gift of the righteous shoot from the stump of Jesse. In this season and in all times, we celebrate the gift of the Savior. As we worship here, we ask that you touch our hearts and teach us mercy, kindness, and love for you and for one another. Enter our hearts and make us yours.

Call to Confession
We have been given instruction for how to live and serve our LORD, but we have not lived up to that instruction fully. We have been taught to live with one another in harmony, but we have not loved our neighbors or our God in the way we are intended. We turn to God and ask for forgiveness and true repentance.

Prayer of Confession
LORD God, you are all grace. You have told us from ancient times what you expect from us as a people, and we have forgotten and ignored your statutes. We have caused disharmony with one another. We have hurt one another and ourselves. We ask that you turn us from our destructive paths that we may return to abide by your instruction for us.

Assurance of Forgiveness
Rejoice all people! Christ has come and rules above all the nations and all powers on earth. He has come to offer salvation to all, and all who come to him are forgiven for their misdeeds. Rejoice greatly!

Offertory Invitation
The root from the stump of Jesse is to be a righteous judge for the poor and an advocate for the meek. As the body of Christ in the world, we, to the best of our ability, should serve those purposes, too. One way we care for the poor is through our united giving, that the church may be a place of hope and mercy for all people. Let us give generously, even as we have received gratefully.

Offertory Prayer
We recognize that only a small portion of all the gifts we receive from your hands are represented here. We pray that these gifts would be used in ways that are pleasing to you, and that you would increase our faith that we may be willing to give more of ourselves, our lives, and our gifts to your people. Amen.

Benediction
The root of Jesse has come. He is the hope of all people. May we go this day sharing that hope with all we have and all we are and all we will be. Amen.

Third Sunday of Advent

Scripture
Isaiah 35:1-10
Psalm 146:5-10 (Or Luke 1:46b-55)
James 5:7-10
Matthew 11:2-11

Call to Worship
One: Happy are those whose help is the God of Jacob.
Happy are those whose hope is in the LORD our God.
Many: God has made the heavens and the earth.
God made all that is in them and remains faithful forever.
One: God executes justice for the oppressed,
God gives food to the hungry.
Many: The LORD sets the prisoners free.
The LORD opens the eyes of the blind.
One: the LORD lifts up those who are bowed down.
God watches over the righteous, the strangers, the orphans and widows.
Many: The LORD will reign forever and ever.
The LORD is our God for all generations! Praise God!

Invocation
LORD, God, we pray with all those who have come before. May our souls magnify you. We rejoice in our Savior, because you have looked on us with favor. Meet us this day and every day, guiding our hearts into deeper, more incredible relationship with you.

Call to Confession
We affirm every time that we pray the Lord's Prayer that we wish to be forgiven in the same way that we forgive others. Our hearts are not easily moved to forgiveness. Our bodies are not easily led from temptation. We have participated in many sins, as a group and as individuals. Let us confess those now before God.

Prayer of Confession
Forgiving God, we pray for your guidance in our lives. We have been slow to forgive. We have been quick to jump at

opportunities that benefit us but hurt others of your people. We have followed after all kinds of things that do not satisfy. Forgive us where we have made mistakes and help us to be a loving and forgiving people.

Assurance of Forgiveness
The Mighty One has done great things for all of us. God has shown us mercy and has provided for us a way to be made clean even in the midst of all our sins. The Christ came into the world that we might be forgiven through him. Thanks to God for this wonderful gift of life!

Offertory Invitation
In Mary's prayer, Mary affirms God's desire that the weak would be made strong, the poor would be made rich, the hungry would be made full. These are at the heart of our offering. We give that God's people throughout the world would be lifted up. We give that our world may become more like God's true kingdom.

Offertory Prayer
We are thankful for all the gifts that we have received from you, gracious God. We have taken moments here to give back a portion of that which has been given to us. We pray that this would only be one time of giving, and that our hearts may also be moved to give of all the gifts we have received from you that the world may know the love and good news of Jesus the Christ. Amen.

Benediction
The spirit of the LORD, the giver of life and salvation, be with all of you this day and every day. May your lives shine the light of Christ that the world may know the great joy we have in Christ Jesus. Go and shine for all to see. Amen.

Fourth Sunday of Advent

Scripture
Isaiah 7:10-16
Psalm 80:1-7, 17-19
Romans 1:1-7
Matthew 1:18-25

Call to Worship
One: A sign is given to the world.
The young woman is with child and shall bear a son.
Many: He shall be called Emmanuel.
Emmanuel, meaning God is with us!
One: The Christ is coming, the very God in the person of a human.
We proclaim his birth and celebrate his coming!
Many: We sing as the angels sang,
Glory to God and on Earth peace to all people.
One: We invite the Christ to live among us and within us,
Teaching us to be true children of God.
Many: Glory be to God, the great Trinity,
Both now and forevermore! Amen!

Invocation
The prophet Isaiah sent the word. The angel proclaimed to Joseph the wondrous news. We are to receive a new one, a messiah, the one who will be ruler of us all. We pray, God, that you would prepare our hearts and minds to allow the Christ to be with us and be in us. Make us your own. Amen.

Call to Confession
We call upon the Spirit of the LORD to come to us and save us, just as the psalmist did in ages past. We recognize some of our sinfulness, and we ask the Spirit to come to us and show us our sinful ways, that we may know how to repent and how to live as faithful disciples of Christ. We turn now in repentance to God in Christ's name.

Prayer of Confession
Through Christ you have offered grace to your people. We come before you, asking to receive that grace, and truly sorry for the ways that we have sinned against you and against your creation. We participate in sins of our communities, our societies, and in our own individual sins. Cleanse us and help us to step rightly all our days.

Assurance of Forgiveness
All who belong to Christ have received the grace that Christ offered through his atonement for all of us. When we dedicate ourselves to following Christ, remembering our faults and resolving to sin no more, that grace covers us more fully than the depth of our sins. Thanks to God for this wondrous gift!

Offertory Invitation
Our gifts have all been given through the hand of the great LORD and creator of all. Everything we have ultimately belongs to God. Let us give back to God a great measure of what we have received in thanksgiving for God's gifts and in faithful response to the master of the universe.

Offertory Prayer
We place these gifts before you, Creator. We trust in your power and wisdom to use these gifts in the best possible ways. We dedicate them fully to that end, that we may give your love to your people wherever they are found, the world over. Amen.

Benediction
Grace to you and peace from God the Father and the Lord Jesus Christ and the great Holy Spirit. May the great one-in-three go with you this day and guide and direct you in all your days. Amen.

Nativity of the Lord

Scripture
Isaiah 9:2-7
Psalm 96
Titus 2:11-14
Luke 2:1-14 (15-20)

Call to Worship
One: Sing to the LORD a new song!
Sing to the LORD, all the earth!
Many: Sing to the LORD, bless God's name.
Tell of God's salvation from day to day!
One: Declare God's glory among all nations.
Declare God's marvelous works among all the peoples!
Many: For the LORD is greatly to be praised.
The LORD God is to be revered above all things.
One: Honor and majesty are before God,
Strength and beauty are within God's sanctuary.
Many: Ascribe to the LORD the glory due to God's name.
Worship the LORD in holy splendor, all the earth!

Invocation
Wonderful, giving and loving God, you are great beyond measure. We worship you for your love for humanity, for in love you sent our Lord, Jesus. He has come to redeem the people. He has come to give us salvation. He has come to free us from our bondage to sin. We thank you, LORD, for the gift of the son, and we return our love to you in this time of worship. Meet us here, LORD. Amen.

Call to Confession
It is for our redemption that the savior of the universe has come. We are unable to save ourselves. We have fallen short, and we must call to mind the ways that we have sinned against God and against others, that we might confess those sins and receive forgiveness. Let us pray together.

Prayer of Confession
Merciful LORD, God of all the universe, we confess that we have sinned against you and against our sisters and brothers. We have participated in the ways that societies have pre-judged your children, ways that have led to economic disparity the world over, ways that have caused wars and famine and injustice. Help us to recognize all our sinfulness, and help us to give our lives to you in humble repentance.

Assurance of Forgiveness
The grace of God has appeared, bringing salvation to all! The gift of the Lord, Jesus the Christ, is the gift of salvation, the gift of redemption, the gift of forgiveness for all of humanity. Praise be to God!

Offertory Invitation
As we celebrate the greatest gift ever given to humanity, we must take a moment to think of our own giving back to God. What can we give? We can never repay the gifts of God, but we can give all we can so that others may know the gift of the Christ. We give gladly, that we may serve fully.

Offertory Prayer
As we return these gifts to you, Lord God, we ask that you would use them in the ways that you determine are best for your world. We need wisdom, we need guidance, and we need your help to do as much with these gifts as we possibly can. Bless these your gifts, and bless us as we do our best to use them faithfully. Amen.

Benediction
Now, go, telling the world of the wondrous news from Bethlehem. A savior is born. The child is here. We, like those shepherds, must go and make known what we have learned about the child. May we amaze others as those shepherds did long ago. Amen.

First Sunday After Christmas

Scripture
Isaiah 63:7-9
Psalm 148
Hebrews 2:10-18
Matthew 2:13-23

Call to Worship
One: The LORD's works are gracious and abundant.
The acts of the LORD are praiseworthy.
Many: The LORD has done great things for us.
God has shown us great favor, according to God's mercy.
One: Out of the abundance of God's steadfast love,
God said we are surely God's people.
Many: God proclaimed us to be children who will deal in truth,
And God became for us our salvation.
One: In all our distress it was no angel or messenger who came to us.
It was the presence of God that saved us.
Many: In God's love and pity we were redeemed.
God lifted up and carried the people from times of old.

Invocation
You called us into being, Great and Powerful One, and you made us in your image. We praise you for the great works you have done among us. In this season, as we celebrate the gift of the Christ child, we are reminded of the grace you showed in giving us an advocate. You made Jesus a human like us so that we could be redeemed through him. We thank you and we worship you. Amen.

Call to Confession
All people have at some time been drawn to sinfulness. Some, like Herod, sinned in their greed for power. Others in desire for money, and still others in innumerable ways. Humanity is sinful, and we are all part of that sinfulness. We come to God now to confess.

Prayer of Confession
Gracious One, we are a part of the world. We are drawn into its ways. We have fallen for its promises and we have pursued the things that we think the world has to offer. And we have done this at the expense of our relationship with you. Forgive us, we pray. Draw us back to proper relationship with you and with others and help us to live the lives you call us to live.

Assurance of Forgiveness
The author of Hebrews tells us that Jesus is our pioneer of salvation. It is through Jesus we receive salvation, and Jesus is not ashamed to call us sisters and brothers. Through the Christ we have the ability to be made whole, even though we recognize our sinfulness. It is in Christ that we have our **Assurance of Forgiveness**.

Offertory Invitation
The gift of the Christ is beyond any gift we could imagine to give back to God. Yet we must do our best to give of our best to God, because God is the source of all our being. We give that God's work can be done here in our lives and in the life of the church. Let us give all we have and all we are.

Offertory Prayer
Redeemer of all, our offerings are one measure of our faithfulness to you. We give to you that we may do our part to bring your healing to the world. Please accept these offerings and bless them that they may make great changes in this world, that it may better resemble your coming kingdom. Amen.

Benediction
In Christ, the LORD has raised up a horn for the people. As we leave this place, let us draw close to God and let us exalt God's name to the end of the earth. Praise the LORD! Amen.

Second Sunday after Christmas Day

Scripture
Jeremiah 31:7-14
Psalm 147:12-20
Ephesians 1:3-14
John 1:(1-9), 10-18

Call to Worship
One: The Word has come!
Thanks be to God!
Many: The very Word of God has come among us.
We welcome the Christ into the world.
One: The LORD is bringing all the people together.
God will gather all God's people from far away.
Many: They shall come together and sing praises.
They will eat and have their fill.
One: Peace shall reign over all the people.
The people of the LORD will be redeemed.
Many: Thanks to God for this great and glorious gift.
Thanks to God for the redemption of creation.

Invocation
Lord God, you have sent the Word into the world. Before you even sent the Christ, you knew what it would do for us, and you also knew what the cost would be. We are overwhelmed when we realize this wonderful thing done for us. May Christ's spirit be with us here, that we may learn of him. May Christ's will become our will. Help us to give back the love and praise you require. Amen.

Call to Confession
We have been called as adopted children of the most high God. Even though we live in this call, we have not been able to follow God's laws and desires perfectly. We have sinned against God and against our fellow humans. Let us humbly confess and repent.

Prayer of Confession
We confess, awesome God, that, even though we call ourselves your people, we have stumbled along the way. We have forgotten to give you your due. Our hearts have been far from you and your people. Instead, we have focused on ourselves and our worldly desires. Forgive us, we pray, and help us to be made new in your love.

Assurance of Forgiveness
Through Christ we have redemption. We have the forgiveness of our trespasses according to Christ's grace. We have been adopted as children of the most high God and through Christ have been redeemed. Let us rejoice.

Offertory Invitation
God has lavished upon us grace after grace, blessing after blessing. As part of our worship, we turn our minds to what we can give back to God. Through our offering, we are to give our very best back to God gratefully thanking God for all we have received.

Offertory Prayer
We dedicate our gifts and ourselves to Christ in this time of worship. We pray that you would shower the people with blessings through the worshipers gathered here and through the gifts we have returned to you. May the world see love through us. Amen.

Benediction
Blessed be the God and Father of the Lord Jesus Christ!
God has blessed us all in Christ with every spiritual blessing in the heavenly places.
Let us live our lives in response to that love.

Epiphany

Scripture
Isaiah 60:1-6
Psalm 72:1-7, 10-14
Ephesians 3:1-12
Matthew 2:1-12

Call to Worship
One: Arise, shine; for your light has come!
The glory of the LORD has risen upon you!
Many: The glory of the LORD shall be known to all.
The light shall shine for all to see.
One: Although darkness shall cover the earth,
Thick darkness shall cover the people,
Many: The LORD will arise upon the people,
and God's glory will appear over us.
One: Nations come to bring their wealth.
They bring their wonders to give to the LORD.
Many: They shall bring gold and frankincense,
They shall proclaim the praise of the LORD.

Invocation
Draw all people to yourself, Loving God. May your desires be the desires of your people. Help us to recognize you in all the world, within the church, and far away from the influence of the church. Meet us here in this place and claim us as your own. Amen.

Call to Confession
The psalmist declares that the LORD delivers the needy when they call. The LORD has pity on the weak and poor. The LORD redeems those who live in violence and oppression. These are the desires of the LORD. How close have our hearts been to these desires?

Prayer of Confession
Great One, when we remember your promises to the poor and needy, when we think of your desire to rescue those in oppression and amidst violence, we realize that we have focused so much on

ourselves we cannot always even see those needs. Forgive us and help us to use your love to do your work in this world.

Assurance of Forgiveness
In our humility, God hears our plea for forgiveness. In our repentance, God will forgive our inability to be all we have been asked to be. When we humbly repent, we are forgiven. Praise God for this promise!

Offertory Invitation
Kings from far away traveled a great distance to give gifts to the Christ child. They gave gifts of great value to the young king. Our gifts are also offered to Christ and they, too, should be of the best that we have. Let us give all we can.

Offertory Prayer
Christ take these gifts and use them to fulfill your purposes. We dedicate them to you and pray that they may heal people in our area and throughout the world. Since you have loved so much, please use these gifts to spread that love to all we can reach.

Benediction
As we continue to follow the star of Jesus, know that Christ can make all things new.
As we leave this sanctuary, take Christ's love to all you meet.

First Sunday after Epiphany
Baptism of the Lord

Scripture
Isaiah 42:1-9
Psalm 29
Acts 10:34-43
Matthew 3:13-17

Call to Worship
One: Jesus was baptized by John,
Beginning his public ministry.
Many: We who were baptized are also called,
We are called to minister to others in the world.
One: God has called us to be witnesses;
We are to witness to the good news of Christ.
Many: In worship we are renewed to tell the news.
In worship, we are empowered by the Spirit.
One: Let us enter into worship with gladness,
Let us worship God with thanksgiving!
Many: God has brought us here and claimed us.
Thanks be to the great Trinity!

Invocation
Great and wonderful Sacred One, in our baptisms you claimed us as your people. You have sent your Holy Spirit to be with the people of this world. Send your Spirit anew today. Energize us; refresh us. Meet us here, in this time of worship. Ignite our hearts to serve you, to serve others, and to tell of your great works of love to all the world.

Call to Confession
The LORD has called us in righteousness, but even when we have tried our best, we have not perfectly heeded that call. We are not righteous. We envy, we judge, we cause pain to one another. We forget God and go our own way. Let us confess the things that have kept us from the righteousness God has called us toward.

Prayer of Confession
Our world is broken, Holy One. We witness devastation, pain, racism, sexism, and many other kinds of prejudice. Your people have participated in these things, sowing hate instead of love, spreading disdain and fear instead of understanding and justice. Forgive these, our faults, and grant that we may walk in your way.

Assurance of Forgiveness
Peter assured those to whom he preached that those who fear God and do what is right are acceptable to God. He goes on to say that all the prophets testify that everyone who believes in Christ received forgiveness of sins through Christ's name. Repent, and you are forgiven. Thanks be to God!

Offertory Invitation
In this time of offering, we have an opportunity to respond faithfully to the gift of the Christ and the gift of God's Spirit into this world. How can we respond to such a wonderful love? One possible way we can respond faithfully is by giving generously of ourselves, our time, our talents, and our treasure.

Offertory Prayer
Grace giver, we are aware that our gifts are only a small portion of the blessings we have received. Yet, we still approach you, praying to have our gifts blessed, that they may be a blessing to your world. Lord, take these gifts and use them where you find them most needed. Amen.

Benediction
Christ is the son, the beloved one of God.
In Christ, God proclaimed to be greatly pleased.
There is none like Jesus the Christ.
Let us go forth into the world proclaiming the wonders of Christ's love.
Amen.

Second Sunday after the Epiphany

Scripture
Isaiah 49:1-7
Psalm 40:1-11
1 Corinthians 1:1-9
John 1:29-42

Call to Worship
One: As we patiently wait for the LORD,
The LORD will incline to us and hear our cry.
Many: God places a new song in our mouths, A song of praise;
Many will see and put their trust in the LORD.
One: God's wondrous deeds have been multiplied to us.
None compares to our God!
Many: If we were to try to tell of all God's wonders to us,
They would be more than we could ever count.
One: Delight, all people, to do God's will.
May God's law be written upon our hearts.
Many: Let us speak of God's faithfulness and salvation.
May God's steadfast love and faithfulness keep us safe forever.

Invocation
Ground of all being, you have called your people to be a servant people, serving you and serving your creation. Plant seeds of service in our hearts. Water those seeds within us that they may grow and become our all-consuming call in the world. Let us truly be your people and worship you alone as our God. Amen.

Call to Confession
The people of God have been called to be a light to the nations. We are to be the heralds of God's power, God's wonder, and God's glory to the ends of the earth. Many times we are sidetracked on our quest to be God's people. Let us confess where we have fallen short.

Prayer of Confession
You are the light of the world, Great and Holy God. We are meant to reflect that light to all those around us. But we have

been drawn to other lights—false idols in your world. We have followed our own way, deceiving others, pushing the weak aside. Forgive us and help us to focus ourselves solely on you.

Assurance of Forgiveness
John said of Jesus, "Here comes the Lamb of God who takes away the sins of the world!" It is this Jesus we proclaim, and it is in this Jesus we believe. The Lamb of God is faithful to take away every sin of those who love and trust in him. As we dedicate ourselves to Christ and confess our sins, they are forgiven.

Offertory Invitation
All we have and all we are intended to be used for God's purposes in the world. During these moments of worship, we attempt to give faithfully that God's purposes may be foremost in our hearts and in the work of God's church. Let us give generously that the world may see the light of the nations in us.

Offertory Prayer
Nothing we could give could ever be enough in return for all God has given us. We pray that God would receive these gifts from a grateful and loving community. We pray that God may give us wisdom to use these gifts in the best way to show God's light to all around. Come, Lord, and bless our efforts. Amen.

Benediction
Grace to you and peace from God the Father and Jesus Christ our Lord!
God is faithful; By God we were called into the fellowship of the Son,
Jesus Christ our Lord.
May we live and move and have our being in Christ alone.
Amen.

Third Sunday after the Epiphany

Scripture
Isaiah 9:1-4
Psalm 27:1, 4-9
1 Corinthians 1:10-18
Matthew 4:12-23

Call to Worship
One: The LORD is my light and my salvation;
Whom then shall I fear?
Many: The LORD is the stronghold of our lives.
We shall be afraid of nothing.
One: One thing I have asked; one thing I seek,
To live in the house of the LORD all the days of my life.
Many: We seek to behold the beauty of the LORD,
We desire to greet the LORD in the temple.
One: In the day of trouble, the LORD will shelter me.
God will conceal me under the cover of God's tent.
Many: The LORD will set me high upon a rock.
I will sing and make melody to the LORD over all.

Invocation
"Come," our hearts tell us. "Come and seek the face of the LORD." Gracious one, it is you we seek, it is you we desire, it is communion with you that we long for. Show us your face, grant us your peace, and fill us with your love as we turn our praises to you. Let us meet you in fullness of body, mind, and spirit here.

Call to Confession
The people who have walked in darkness have seen a great light. We all walk in darkness at times, and when we step toward the light, it can give us the ability to see our sinfulness better. Let us confess our sins before a loving God.

Prayer of Confession
Giver of Life, we have turned away from your light. We have treated ourselves badly, we have treated one another badly, and we have ignored your will for our world. Help us to see our ways

better, help us to recognize where they differ from your ways, and cause us to truly repent that our new ways may be the ways you desire in us.

Assurance of Forgiveness
The light that shines on all the world has come to us. We not only recognize our sinfulness when we approach the light, we are cleansed by that same light. Thanks be to God for the cleansing, atoning work of the Son, Jesus the Christ.

Offertory Invitation
Jesus simply asked others to follow, and they dropped whatever they were doing and went with him. As we worship in the giving of our offering, may we be like those first disciples, willing to give all we have to the glory of Jesus, the Christ.

Offertory Prayer
Thank you, great One, for the gifts we have received from you. You have blessed us beyond our worth, beyond our ability to comprehend. Accept these sacrifices from us now. May they be blessed by you and used for your glory in all the earth. Amen.

Benediction
As we leave this place, let us be united in the same mind and the same purpose,
And that purpose is the will of the Lord, Jesus the Christ in our communities,
In our circles of influence,
and throughout the world.
All glory to Christ!
Amen.

Fourth Sunday after the Epiphany

Scripture
Micah 6:1-8
Psalm 15
1 Corinthians 1:18-31
Matthew 5:1-12

Call to Worship
One: We come together proclaiming Jesus, the crucified.
For to us who are being saved, the cross is the power of God.
Many: God's foolishness is wiser than human wisdom.
God's weakness is stronger than human strength.
One: We are called by God to proclaim the gospel message.
All may be saved through Jesus the Messiah.
Many: This message is for all the world,
Salvation is not to be gained through human means.
One: Salvation is only through the one given for us, Christ our Lord,
That we may not boast of ourselves, only of Christ.
Many: He is the very source of life.
Christ Jesus, the wisdom of God and righteousness of the world.

Invocation
Holy Creator, through your wisdom may we become wise. Through your grace may we become saved. Through your love may we learn to love you and your world. We pray that we would be overwhelmed by your Spirit. May it wash us thoroughly, and may it make us yours alone. Amen.

Call to Confession
The pathway to salvation begins with recognizing that we cannot save ourselves. Only through the will of God and the grace given us can we be made whole. Through the grace of God, we may be redeemed, and relying on the grace of God we now ask for forgiveness for our sins.

Prayer of Confession
You have told us mortals what is good, O LORD. We are to do justice, love kindness, and walk humbly with you. We are at best imperfect at this and perhaps even sometimes ignore the ways we should embrace. Forgive our sins and draw us into repentance and true forgiveness of one another.

Assurance of Forgiveness
Christ is faithful to forgive when we are faithful to repent. The grace of God extends from the heavens to the farthest reaches of the universe. We only need to give ourselves back to God, humbly, offering kindness and justice to one another to be forgiven.
Thank you, Great One!

Offertory Invitation
The gifts from the eternal one are wondrous and incredible. In gratefulness for those gifts, we are called to give of ourselves to bless others the world over and to extend Christ's reach in this world. Let us give generously that God may be glorified!

Offertory Prayer
Accept these gifts from a grateful and loving fellowship, wondrous God. Give us strength and wisdom to use all our gifts in ways that help others to know of your good news—the good news of the salvation of the entire creation. May our gifts and all we have be a part of the announcement of your wonder.

Benediction
Go, proclaiming Christ crucified...
A stumbling block to some,
but the power and wisdom of God to us who are called to hear the good news.
Praise be to God forever.
Amen.

Fifth Sunday after the Epiphany

Scripture
Isaiah 58:1-9a (9b-12)
Psalm 112:1-9 (10)
1 Corinthians 2:1-12 (13-16)
Matthew 5:13-20

Call to Worship
One: Praise the LORD! Happy are those who fear the LORD,
Those who greatly delight in God's commandments.
Many: The generation of the upright will be blessed.
Their righteousness endures forever.
One: They rise in the darkness as a light for the upright.
They are gracious, merciful, and righteous.
Many: The righteous will never be moved.
They will be remembered forever.
One: Lord, may our praises rise to you this day,
That we, too, may be counted with the righteous.
Many: Grant that we may love what you love.
Make our will one with yours.

Invocation
Maker of us all, we know that you plumb the depths of our being. You know us more intimately than any other could ever know us. Hear the songs of our hearts today, singing praises to you and wonder to your majesty. Open our lives to your Spirit that we may become fully yours. Amen.

Call to Confession
We are the salt of the earth. If salt has lost its saltiness, it becomes good for nothing. As a body and as individuals, through our sins we have compromised what it is that makes us different from the rest of the world. Let us confess those sins that we might receive forgiveness.

Prayer of Confession
Spirit over all, you have moved in us to love you, to love others, to loose the bonds of injustice, to let the oppressed go free, and to

break every yoke. We have, instead, affirmed yokes and tied unjust bonds ourselves. Forgive our evil ways and lead us in the path of righteousness.

Assurance of Forgiveness
Jesus assured us that those who ask for forgiveness will receive it. You are forgiven this day. As we continue in our lives, let us do our very best to honor our own repentance this day. With God's help, let us go and sin no more!

Offertory Invitation
The psalmist writes of the righteous ones, "They had distributed freely, they have given to the poor. Their righteousness endures forever." Can we count ourselves with these righteous? Let us give of ourselves freely and let us honor God by caring for the poor.

Offertory Prayer
Lord God, we offer these gifts to you this day. May they be multiplied in your hands. May we be instruments of your righteousness by giving to the poor and needy, and freely distributing the blessings you have given us for the good of your world. Amen.

Benediction
You are the light of the world.
A city built on a hill cannot be hidden.
Therefore, shine your light before others, so they may see your good works, and bless God in heaven.
Amen.

Sixth Sunday after the Epiphany

Scripture
Deuteronomy 30:15-20
Psalm 119:1-8
1 Corinthians 3:1-9
Matthew 5:21-37

Call to Worship
One: Set before us this day are the ways of life and prosperity.
Also before us are the ways of death and adversity.
Many: We choose to obey the commandments of the LORD.
We pray that God will bless and increase us.
One: Choose this day to love and serve the LORD your God.
Obey God and hold fast to the LORD.
Many: God's commands mean good for us.
We seek God with our hearts.
One: Happy are all those who serve the LORD.
The LORD honors those who walk in God's way.
Many: May the LORD guide us and keep us steady.
May we be found in God's grace!

Invocation
LORD God of all generations, you blessed our ancestors in the faith as they entered into their new land. Even when they chose to disobey your commands, you were faithful to your promises. Help us to obey all your ordinances and honor you with our very lives. Come to us this hour that we may set aside our ways and follow you alone. Amen.

Call to Confession
With all of the love we have for God through Christ, we remain people of the flesh. As such, we are unable to live perfect lives in the way that Christ did. We are people within the world and are influenced by it. Let us confess the ways we have fallen short of God's call.

Prayer of Confession
Although you set before us life and prosperity, death and

adversity, Perfect One, we find ourselves choosing poorly more often than we would like. We follow the ways of this world, choosing to forget our vows to you or unknowingly harming your creation. Forgive the ways we have failed and help us to choose life more often.

Assurance of Forgiveness
Christ came into the world in order to offer forgiveness to creation for the way we have fallen. Christ knows that we are an imperfect people, and he came to offer us salvation anyway. When we call upon the name of our Lord, we are forgiven. Thanks be to God.

Offertory Invitation
This time of worship is set aside for our offering. We offer gifts of our treasures to God, but we also remind ourselves and one another that our gifts must include ourselves and our hearts as well. Let us give, gratefully glorifying God for all we have been given.

Offertory Prayer
Our offering is here before you, Great One. We can give, and we hope we have given with your blessing, but we recognize that even our best efforts rely on you for growth. Take these gifts, help them to grow, and cause them to light this world. Amen.

Benediction
We are God's servants, working together.
Let us go into the world, working for the love of God and the salvation of Christ for all people.
Amen.

Seventh Sunday after the Epiphany

Scripture
Leviticus 19:1-2, 9-18
Psalm 119:33-40
1 Corinthians 3:10-11, 16-23
Matthew 5:38-48

Call to Worship
One: We are to be holy,
Because the LORD our God is holy.
Many: We are to remember the poor and care for them,
We are to be certain not to greedily hold to all our possessions.
One: We who love the LORD's ways are to remember the law.
We shall care for all those in our land with love and respect.
Many: May the LORD grant that we have understanding.
May that understanding help us to learn to honor God.
One: The LORD commands that we are to forgive our neighbors.
When we forgive, we, too, are forgiven.
Many: We shall remember to love our neighbors as ourselves.
We learn through God's grace to give ourselves to love.

Invocation
God above all, you call us to things that seem impossible. We are to love those who hate us. We are to give even after much has been taken from us. We cannot be faithful to these commands without your help and guidance. Renew your Spirit's claim on our hearts this day that we may better follow you.

Call to Confession
The wisdom of the wisest person is as foolishness to God. How can any human, then, live according to the ways God has instructed? We all fall short of God's perfect way. Recognizing this, we turn to God in prayer for forgiveness and renewed wholeness.

Prayer of Confession
Love is not as easy for us as we would like, God of wonders. Greed comes easily. Anger overwhelms us. Self-preservation

causes us to treat others as objects rather than beautiful creations made in your image. Forgive our human sinfulness and help us to walk the better way.

Assurance of Forgiveness
When we recognize our sinfulness, and when we realize that our greatest ways are nothing compared to the way of God, then we can approach God with true repentance of heart. When we do this, God is always faithful to forgive. All praise to the great Three-in-One for these blessings!

Offertory Invitation
If we love those who love us, what reward do we have? If we give only what is left over, will we be called blessed? Our offering is a chance to show our great faithfulness to God by giving more than we think we can afford. Let us give, grateful for the gifts we have received.

Offertory Prayer
Our gifts are here before you, LORD God. We offer them to you, praising you for your blessings, and praying that they may be used by ourselves and others to reach out to your people near and far. You have given so much, may the gifts we return show your blessings to others. Amen.

Benediction
All things, all people, life and death and the present and future belong to Christ, and Christ belongs to God. As we go into the world, let us carry the love of Christ to the unloved and unlovable. Amen.

Eighth Sunday after the Epiphany

Scripture
Isaiah 49:8-16a
Psalm 131
1 Corinthians 4:1-5
Matthew 6:24-34

Call to Worship
One: The LORD is calling together all of God's people;
All the people will come, from the four corners of the world.
Many: God says that the people are inscribed on the palm of God's hand.
We can never be forgotten or forsaken.
One: We praise a God who lifts up the fallen.
We serve a God who feeds the hungry and frees the enslaved.
Many: None shall hunger or thirst, none shall be struck by sun or wind.
God will comfort the people.
One: The LORD will lead the people,
And by springs of water God will guide them.
Many: We break forth with all the world into singing!
The LORD has shown faithfulness to the people again and again!

Invocation
LORD, calm and quiet our souls. Give us expectant spirits and open hearts to encounter you this day. You have sent your Spirit to be among us. You have redeemed us through your Son. You have called us together in worship in this hour. Renew our desire to be yours now and refresh our souls with your merciful and powerful touch. Amen.

Call to Confession
Paul reminds us that we cannot judge one another. In fact, we cannot judge ourselves. Even if we are unaware of anything that is against us, we cannot simply declare ourselves to be righteous. Instead, we are reminded that it is God alone who judges. With this in mind, let us pray for forgiveness.

Prayer of Confession
We may realize many ways that we are sinful in your sight, Great God, but even if we do, we are unable to judge our own lives. That belongs to you alone. Knowing that we cannot be perfect as Christ was perfect, we ask for forgiveness of sins known and unknown, deeds done and left undone. Forgive us and help us to rely on your righteousness alone.

Assurance of Forgiveness
We have come to God confessing our sins. We have admitted that we are unrighteous people in need of salvation. We have even confessed that we do not know the extent of our own sins. God has promised when we humbly repent and come to God seeking pardon, God is faithful to forgive. We celebrate that forgiveness this and every day.

Offertory Invitation
We cannot serve two masters. Either we serve God, or we serve something else. It is not an option for the Christian to honor money before Christ. We bear this in mind as we give of all we have received back to God.

Offertory Prayer
Our lives and our treasures are yours, O God. Help us to learn to not worry about what we will have or eat or drink, but help us to care about the things you care about. Remind us how to follow your way, and bless us as we try to use our offerings to do that. Amen.

Benediction
Seek first the kingdom of God,
and seek after God's righteousness.
Then all the things you worry about today will be given to you by our Gracious God.
Glory to the Creator, Savior, and Holy Spirit!
Amen.

Ninth Sunday after the Epiphany

Scripture
Deuteronomy 11:18-21, 26-28
Psalm 31:1-5, 19-24
Romans 1:16-17, 3:22b-28 (29-31)
Matthew 7:21-29

Call to Worship
One: The ways of the LORD are righteous and good.
We who love the LORD are called to follow in God's ways.
Many: We will place the words of the LORD on our hearts and souls.
We will bind them as a sign upon our lives.
One: The LORD promises blessings for those who obey,
Blessings for all people who obey the LORD's commandments.
Many: How abundant is the goodness that God has for those who trust.
God's wonderful grace extends to all who love the LORD.
One: Be strong, and let your hearts take courage,
All you who wait upon the LORD.
Many: We await God's mercy and love with anticipation.
How great is our God in all the earth!

Invocation
In our times of need, Sacred One, you are faithful to hear the calls of your people. In this hour, an hour of our need for you, bless us with your wondrous presence. Enter into our hearts and minds once more. Write your words on our souls and cause us to become truly and only yours. Amen.

Call to Confession
Scripture tells us that all have sinned and all fall short of the glory of God. We know this to be true in our individual lives and within our communities. The laws of God are often far from us. Our will is often for our own good instead of for the good of God and God's children. Let us humbly ask God for forgiveness.

Prayer of Confession
We have fallen short of your glory, great God. We have lost sight of our purpose, and we have gone our own way. We have not loved you as we should. We have not loved one another. We have judged, hated, disdained, and envied one another. We have neglected your way. Rescue us once again in your faithfulness.

Assurance of Forgiveness
We are justified not through our works, but through our faith. When we declare to God our repentance for deeds we have done or for other ways we have sinned against God and neighbor, we are declaring our faith that God can and will forgive. Through that faith, we are forgiven. All praise to God!

Offertory Invitation
We come not only to hear the words of Christ, but to act upon those words. One faithful response to the words of Christ is to give all we can to heal the sick, comfort the bereaved, feed the hungry, clothe the naked, and in many other ways care for God's people. Let us give because we have been called.

Offertory Prayer
Nothing we could give could ever be enough until we give ourselves. We pray that the gifts we have given this day may be a blessing to your people. May we have hearts for giving, so that many throughout your world may be healed. Amen.

Benediction
The words of Christ are a great blessing to the believer,
Even if they are sometimes hard to hear.
We still are astonished at Christ's teaching.
May we go as the wise, hearing the words of Christ,
And putting them to action in our lives.
Amen.

Transfiguration Sunday

Scripture
Exodus 24:12-18
Psalm 2 *or Psalm 99*
2 Peter 1:16-21
Matthew 17:1-9

Call to Worship
One: The glory of the LORD is found in all the world.
The majesty of God is manifest in all creation.
Many: It is like a devouring fire in the sight of God's people.
It overwhelms and awes all who see.
One: The LORD rules over all the earth.
Kings and rulers have no power compared to God.
Many: The LORD has set the holy one as ruler of all.
The Christ is enthroned forever.
One: Serve the LORD and take refuge in God.
Bow down to the holy one.
Many: We worship the God of all, the beloved Son,
and the Holy Spirit. Praise the great three-in-one!

Invocation
Great Trinity, we stand in awe of your mighty power and your great mercy. You are unfathomable wonder. Draw us close in this worship time. Empty our spirits so they can be filled with your Spirit. Deeply inspire us that we may love and serve all creation in your name.

Call to Confession
Like Peter, we sometimes interfere with our own moments of inspiration and holiness. Even when we intend good, we can cause imperfections or grief with our actions. We cannot see all God can see, and because of this we cannot act, even with the best of intentions, in the way God would have us act all of the time. During these moments, we confess our sins before God.

Prayer of Confession
LORD of all things, you know us more intimately than we know

ourselves. You see us perfectly, you know us fully. Help us to understand our own imperfections and forgive us. Give us repentant hearts that we may see our faults, turn from them, and go forward to sin no more.

Assurance of Forgiveness
The Son of God, the Beloved of the LORD, has come into our world to redeem humanity. While we neither deserve this redemption, nor can we work for it, we have been given forgiveness through the atonement of the Christ. God is gracious to forgive, when we turn away from ourselves and listen to the Beloved one. Friends, you are forgiven!

Offertory Invitation
In Christ, God is well pleased. Christ emptied himself, giving of all he had and all he was in order that the creation of the LORD could have salvation. As disciples of Christ, we are to follow in Christ's footsteps. Let us empty ourselves that others the world over may also have salvation.

Offertory Prayer
Our prayer is simple, Great One. We ask that what we have offered here may make a difference for good in your world. May we have wisdom to use our gifts and strength to part with them for the increase of your kingdom. Amen.

Benediction
As you leave this day,
Go in awe of the ruler of all creation,
Go, proclaiming the sovereignty and the love of Christ.
Go, worshiping and telling all of the amazing God we serve.
Amen.

Ash Wednesday

Scripture
Joel 2:1-2, 12-17 or Isaiah 58:1-12
Psalm 51:1-17
2 Corinthians 5:20b-6:10
Matthew 6:1-6, 16-21

Call to Worship
One: We come this day to worship and to atone.
We come to offer ourselves back unto our God.
Many: Our many deeds stand ever before us,
Reminding us of the need for atonement and for healing.
One: God desires fasting, but not the fasting that causes strife.
God does not desire God's people to outwardly mortify themselves.
Many: Instead, God desires a fasting that releases the prisoners.
God desires that our fasting breaks the yoke of oppression.
One: When we share our bread with the poor and cover the naked,
Our light shines forth like the dawn, and our healing is found in the LORD.
Many: May the LORD our God guide us continually and strengthen us.
May God use us to restore the streets and repair the breaches.

Invocation
LORD of all nations, fill this sanctuary with your presence, and fill us, your people, with the desire to do your justice throughout the world. Make our spirits one with yours that we would love your ways. Give us strength and ability to free this world from need and oppression. Amen.

Call to Confession
The LORD knows our sins, even those that we are unable or choose not to see. It is both a need and a privilege to confess our sins before God that we may receive healing. As a congregation and as individuals we offer our prayers to God.

Prayer of Confession
Have mercy on us, O God, according to your steadfast love. Wash us thoroughly from our iniquities and cleanse us from our guilt. We know our sins are ever before us. We know they are more numerous than even we recognize. You are justified in your sentence against us. But we cry out for mercy, trusting in your abundant grace. Save us, Holy One!

Assurance of Forgiveness
The sacrifice that is acceptable to God is a contrite heart and a broken spirit. When we allow ourselves to be broken in humble confession and when we bow before God, God is faithful to forgive. Through the atonement of Christ, we have a gift we could never earn. Thanks to the Great Spirit over all!

Offertory Invitation
Our giving is not an act that is done in order to receive blessing for ourselves. Jesus commands that we not even allow our left hand to see what gifts our right hand is giving. We do not store up treasures on earth where they are destroyed, but rather in heaven where they are eternal. Let us give that others may be blessed and that the name of God may be lifted high!

Offertory Prayer
We have worshiped with our offering, and we pray that our offering is acceptable to you, O LORD. Take what we have, whether it has been given here or not, and use it and all we are to be a beacon of light in this world, a light that reflects your love for creation. Amen.

Benediction
Where your treasure is, there will your heart be also.
Let us store all our treasures in heaven, where they will be for us eternally.
In all things, let us proclaim the LORD our God!
Amen.

First Sunday of Lent

Scripture
Genesis 2:15-17; 3:1-7
Psalm 32
Romans 5:12-19
Matthew 4:1-11

Call to Worship
One: Happy are those whose transgressions are forgiven.
Happy are those whose sin is covered.
Many: In them the LORD imputes no iniquity.
In their spirits, there is no deceit.
One: Let all the faithful offer prayers to our God.
God is a hiding place for those who love the LORD.
Many: The LORD preserves the people in times of trouble.
God surrounds God's children with glad cries of deliverance.
One: The LORD instructs the people in the way they should go.
The faithful follow the ways of the LORD; they are not stubborn.
Many: We will be glad in the LORD and rejoice.
Let the righteous and upright in heart shout for joy to the LORD.

Invocation
You are with us here in this worship space, Holy One. Fill this area with your awe, fill our hearts with your wonder. Awake our senses that we might recognize you in all we see, hear, touch, taste, smell. Let us know you through all we say and do in this time of worship and let us be changed by a true encounter with the one true God. Amen.

Call to Confession
From the beginning of time, humans have rebelled in big and small ways against the boundaries God has set for them. We have not only inherited this rebellion, we have actively participated in it. Let us confess our sins before the God of all.

Prayer of Confession
Incredible Creator, you fashioned humans in your image, but you did not give your sovereignty to humans. In all generations we

have become conceited enough to believe that we can create our own way apart from you. In many ways we have abandoned your word and ignored your commands. Forgive us and help us to do better.

Assurance of Forgiveness
Sin is in the world, but the redeemer of the people of God also came to the world that we might overcome that sin. Jesus the Christ has atoned for all humanity, once for all. When we worship the Christ, when we turn to Christ in faith, we are forgiven and redeemed. Thanks be to God!

Offertory Invitation
How shall we respond to the overwhelming love of God through Jesus the Christ? Is there anything we can give that would be enough? Although we cannot repay, our gifts of our selves are what God requires of the faithful. Let us respond to the great love of God with generous gifts.

Offertory Prayer
These gifts are offered to you, Great One, that your love and your word may extend to the ends of the earth. Help us to have wisdom to use all we offer to you that not a cent, not a talent, not a moment would be wasted as we work toward your goals on this planet. Amen.

Benediction
Jesus responded in the wilderness to temptation by saying:
"Worship the LORD your God and serve only God."
As we leave this place, let us go forward to worship and serve only
The one true master of the universe.
May God's peace be with you all.
Amen.

Second Sunday of Lent

Scripture
Genesis 12:1-4a
Psalm 121
Romans 4:1-5, 13-17
John 3:1-17 *or Matthew 17:1-9*

Call to Worship
One: I lift up my eyes unto the hills,
From where will my help come?
Many: Our help comes from the LORD,
From our God, the maker of heaven and earth.
One: The LORD will not allow your foot to be moved,
God, who keeps you, will never slumber.
Many: The one who keeps Israel will neither slumber nor sleep.
The LORD is our keeper, a shade at our right hand.
One: The sun will not strike you by day, nor the moon by night.
The LORD will keep you from evil; God will keep your life.
Many: The LORD will keep our going out and coming in,
God will preserve us from this time forth and forevermore.

Invocation
Majestic creator of all things, you have promised to preserve us and keep us. We ask for your great blessings in our lives and in the lives of our congregation. May your Spirit meet us here; may we be re-inspired by the newness of your presence among us. Give us a glimpse of your wonder and make us yours. Amen.

Call to Confession
Jesus taught Nicodemus that in order to receive the kingdom of God he must be born from above. This means in part that we replace our human focus with a Godly one. We turn to God, seeking to be forgiven of our sinful ways, that we may continually be renewed with a rebirth from above.

Prayer of Confession
Great God of mercy, we confess that we have sinned against you and against each other. We have caused divisions to come between

us and between ourselves and you. We have guarded our human preoccupation with worldly things and have not allowed ourselves to be changed by your Spirit. Forgive us, we pray, and help us to truly repent.

Assurance of Forgiveness
God loves the world so much that God sent the one and only Son into the world. This was so that the Son could redeem the world, not in order to condemn it. We have no greater assurance of God's desire to forgive God's people than this. Thanks be to God!

Offertory Invitation
Faith was reckoned to Abraham as righteousness. This was a faith in things he could not see, even in things he imagined to be impossible. As we approach the time of giving to God and God's church, let us also give exhibiting faith in things we cannot see. Let us give generously.

Offertory Prayer
You have called us to give, God of Wonders, and we have responded in this time. May our gifts be acceptable to you. Give us wisdom of heart and mind that we may use all our gifts in ways that please you. Amen.

Benediction
Just as Moses lifted up the serpent in the desert,
So shall the Son of Man be lifted in our world,
So that whoever believes in the Christ may have eternal life.
Go now, lifting Christ before you.
Amen.

Third Sunday of Lent

Scripture
Exodus 17:1-7
Psalm 95
Romans 5:1-11
John 4:5-42

Call to Worship
One: Come, let us sing unto the LORD!
Let us make a joyful noise to the rock of our salvation!
Many: We come into the LORD's presence with thanksgiving.
We make joyful noises to God with songs of praise!
One: The LORD our God is a great God,
In God's hands are the depths of all the earth.
Many: The heights of the mountains, the seas,
The dry lands which have been formed by God's hands are all God's.
One: Come, let us worship and bow down before the LORD.
Let us kneel and praise, for the LORD is our God.
Many: We are the people of God's pasture and the sheep of God's hand.
Let us listen this day to God's voice and give praise!

Invocation
Your Spirit is ever with us God, even when we doubt you. Our ancestors doubted, but you still provided all that they needed. Renew our faith in you and in your gentle provision for us and all your people. Make us to be truly your people, trusting in you for all we may ever need. Amen.

Call to Confession
Christ came into the world and gave himself for us while we were still sinners. This shows the great love that God has for God's creation. We receive forgiveness for our sins through the faith we have in God through Christ. We show our faith by admitting our faults before our maker. Let us confess together.

Prayer of Confession
Shepherd of all, we have all strayed, just as sheep sometimes stray from their shepherds. In ways that we recognize, and in many we do not, we have forgotten your calling on our lives and we have chased after things that do not satisfy. We acknowledge our sins before you, and humbly ask that we may receive your forgiveness.

Assurance of Forgiveness
Paul writes that God shows love for us in that while we still were sinners, Christ died for us. The justification that Christ gives to us is ours to receive through the faith that we show in God and that we show in the messiah of the world, Jesus the Christ. When we repent and place our faith in Christ, we are forgiven.

Offertory Invitation
Like the disciples when they wondered about the food that Jesus might have that they did not know about, we often fixate on worldly things while the spiritual is close at hand. As we come to the time of offering, let us put aside our trust in the physical things of the world and give sacrifices that we may glorify our God.

Offertory Prayer
Lord, please accept the sacrifices we have made to your glory in your world. We pray that our greatest dreams of reaching out beyond this congregation may be realized and surpassed by the great power you have to care for your people. Help us to do all we can to help you toward this goal. Amen.

Benediction
As we close this service, go, boasting in God through Jesus the Christ alone,
In whom and through whom we have received our salvation!
Amen.

Fourth Sunday of Lent

Scripture
1 Samuel 16:1-13
Psalm 23
Ephesians 5:8-14
John 9:1-41

Call to Worship
One: The LORD is our shepherd.
We shall not want.
Many: The LORD makes us to lie down in green pastures.
The LORD leads us beside the still waters.
One: God restores our souls
And leads us in straight paths for God's name's sake.
Many: Even though we should walk through the darkest valley, we will fear no evil.
For you are with us; your rod and your staff, they comfort us.
One: You prepare a table before us in the presence of our enemies.
You anoint our heads with oil; our cups overflow.
Many: Surely goodness and mercy shall follow us all the days of our lives,
And we shall live in the house of the LORD our whole lives long.

Invocation
LORD God, maker of the universe, creator of humanity, we know that you look at people differently than we look at ourselves. You do not look on the outward appearance, but on the heart. Send your Spirit to us in this time and renew our hearts for true worship of you. Cleanse us from our iniquities and help us to shine your light into the world. Amen.

Call to Confession
We were once children of darkness. Now the light has shone on us and into us. Because of the light we have received, we are better able to see ways that we are not the people God wants us to be. We can see our sinfulness. We can see our own darkness. Let us confess our sins before God that we may be redeemed.

Prayer of Confession
Beautiful Savior, your desire is for us to follow you in all our days and in all our ways. We want to be people who do these things. But we have not been able to be your perfect people. We have forgotten you in our daily lives. We have become too involved in things that do not honor you and have neglected things that do bring you honor. Forgive us and renew your Spirit within our hearts.

Assurance of Pardon
Everything in the light becomes visible. Now that we have brought ourselves and our misdeeds into the light, now that we have confessed our sinful ways before God, God will be faithful to forgive. We know we are unworthy to receive forgiveness, but God needs only to desire it, and it is done. Thanks be to God!

Offertory Invitation
What things do we have that truly satisfy? Is there anything that can satisfy us in the way that love of God and love of others satisfies? Let us examine our hearts as we bring our offering and give from the love we have of God and people.

Offertory Prayer
Into your hands, Wonderful Creator, we give these gifts. May they be acceptable to you, and may they bring your word to people who would not know you otherwise. Help us to be willing to sacrifice these gifts and many more for the love that we have of you and your son, Jesus the Christ. Amen.

Benediction
Wake up, sleeper!
Rise from the dead!
Christ will shine on you!
Go now, living these words for the master of the universe.
Amen.

Fifth Sunday of Lent

Scripture
Ezekiel 37:1-14
Psalm 130
Romans 8:6-11
John 11:1-45

Call to Worship
One: Out of the depths we cry unto our God.
LORD, hear our voice!
Many: May your ears be attentive to the voice of our supplications!
If you, O LORD, should mark iniquities, who could stand?
One: But there is forgiveness in you, so that you may be revered. Wait for the LORD, may our souls wait, and let us hope in God's word.
Many: Our souls wait for the LORD more than those who watch for the morning.
We have our hope in the LORD.
One: With the LORD there is steadfast love,
With the LORD there is great power to redeem.
Many: It is the LORD who will redeem the people from iniquities. Our hope and trust are in the LORD.

Invocation
We are all like dry bones, waiting on your Spirit to renew us, Great One. Send that Spirit among us this day. May your breath come into this place, into the hidden corners of our hearts and minds. Fill us with your Spirit that we may become alive again, ready to serve you and live lives of sacrifice for your wonder and glory. Amen.

Call to Confession
To set the mind on the flesh is death. Paul reminds us that when we are caught up in the things of this world, when we turn from the true God and replace God with materialism, we can no longer live righteously, but have already accepted the death of sin. Let us confess that we might be healed.

Prayer of Confession
God of Grace re-instill in us the power of our new hearts, the wonder of our new lives, given to us through Jesus the Christ. Forgive the ways that we have resisted Jesus' commands on our lives and restore in us the desire to please you by putting away sinful desire and following you alone.

Assurance of Pardon
If Christ dwells within us, even though the body may be dead through sin, the Spirit gives the life of righteousness. All those who turn to God in humility and offer true repentance for their sinful ways will be forgiven by a faithful God. Thanks be to the great One-in-Three!

Offertory Invitation
We have nothing that truly belongs to us, but all we have belongs to the God of the Universe. Our giving should reflect that knowledge. Let us give all we can that our wonderful God might be revered to the ends of the earth!

Offertory Prayer
These gifts that we return to you this day, Parent God, we pray may be used for their greatest purpose. We desire that the hungry be fed, the naked clothed, the oppressed released. Whatever we have that can be used toward these, your goals revealed in **Scripture**, help us to be faithful to use them. Amen.

Benediction
Jesus said that he is the resurrection and the life.
Those who believe in the Christ, even though they die, will yet live again.
Go now, assured of the blessing you have received through Christ your Lord!
Amen.

Liturgy of the Palms

Scripture
Psalm 188:1-2, 19-29
Matthew 21:1-11

Call to Worship
One: Give thanks to the LORD, for God is good!
God's steadfast love endures forever!
Many: Let the people say, "The LORD's steadfast love endures forever!"
May the LORD open the gates of righteousness to the people.
One: Let us enter God's gate of righteousness and give thanks to the LORD.
Thanks be to God for answering the people and becoming our salvation.
Many: The stone that the builders rejected has become the chief cornerstone.
This is the LORD's doing, and it is marvelous in our eyes.
One: This is the day that the LORD has made,
Let us rejoice and be glad in it!
Many: O give thanks to the LORD, for God is good!
God's steadfast love endures forever!

Invocation
As we invoke your Spirit in this sanctuary, Holy One, we recognize that it is we who are your guests in this place. Thank you for meeting us here and drawing us unto yourself. Release your Spirit into our hearts and minds, filling us with your love, and replacing our humanity with your perfect divinity. Amen.

Call to Confession
All people sin. This is a simple fact of the human condition. As God's people, we choose to work toward a better way, one that is as free from sin as possible. A starting point to a life of grace is the confessing of our sins and the willingness to truly repent. Let us confess those sins and resolve to repent before our God.

Prayer of Confession
God of all power, all wonder, and all grace, when we look upon our lives with eyes of truth, we see many ways that we have sinned against you and against your people. We have not loved you with our whole hearts. We have not respected your ways, nor have we shown love to your people. Forgive us, we pray, and lead us forward in your righteous way.

Assurance of Forgiveness
God's grace and mercy extend to all those who call upon the name of the LORD. As a body and as individuals we have confessed our sins this day, and we have determined to keep from repeating them. In the name of Christ our Savior, we have been forgiven. Thanks be to God.

Offertory Invitation
When Jesus made his entry into Jerusalem, the people laid palm branches on the road and spread their own garments before him. As we enter into our time of offering, let us gratefully and generously lay our treasures at the feet of Jesus the Christ, who came that we might have salvation.

Offertory Prayer
Lord, our gifts are not worthy of you, but we pray that you would accept them anyway. We ask for your blessing on these gifts and on this congregation. Help us to use our treasures and all we have to glorify you near and far.

Benediction
Let us go out shouting,
"Blessed is the King who comes in the name of the LORD!"
For if we do not proclaim Jesus, even the rocks will begin to cry out.
Let's go, proclaiming our Savior.
Amen.

Liturgy of the Passion

Scripture
Isaiah 50:4-9a
Psalm 31:9-16
Philippians 2:5-11
Matthew 26:14-27:66 *or Matthew 27:11-54*

Call to Worship
One: Christ is the Savior, the one who endured the passion for the sake of the people.
Christ is the example of perfect devotion to God.
Many: The LORD God opened Christ's ear, and Christ was not rebellious.
He did not turn away from the cup he was to drink.
One: Christ gave his back to those who struck him.
Christ gave his cheek to those who would pull out his beard.
Many: He did not hide his face from insults or from spitting,
Yet the Lord GOD was Christ's helper, and he did not suffer disgrace.
One: Christ set his face like flint and was not put to shame.
God, the vindicator, was always near.
Many: It is the Lord GOD who was Christ's helper,
There were none who could declare him to be guilty.

Invocation
As we look upon this time of suffering, as we remember your great trials for the sake of humanity, Lord Christ, give us the gift of your Spirit. Help us to gain your morality, help us to know your pure devotion, and grant that we, too, may participate in your victory over death. Bless us in this time of worship that we might have a glimpse of you in your glory. Amen.

Call to Confession
The passion Christ suffered was for the sake of all humanity. All humans have sinned. It was humanity that crucified the ruler of the universe. Let us humbly approach God in confession for the sins we have committed and let us sincerely pray for help to avoid sinfulness in our future.

Prayer of Confession
We are the builders who rejected the chief cornerstone. We are your people who rejected your Son. We are much the same as our ancestors who did not recognize the maker of the very world we live in and sent him to his death. Forgive our lack of understanding. Forgive our arrogance. Forgive our sinful disdain for you and for one another. Forgive us, we pray.

Assurance of Forgiveness
The God of all the cosmos can forgive, even when we have strayed so far as to condemn our own savior. People may be unfaithful, but God is never unfaithful. God has promised to forgive when we come to God in true repentance. Let us rejoice, that, sinful as we are, God has made us clean once again. Rejoice, all people of God!

Offertory Invitation
How can we respond to a gift so wonderful as the gift of the Christ? How can we begin to give back to a God who has given so much for us? We must give of our very hearts, our very lives, our very selves. That is a gift that is acceptable to God.

Offertory Prayer
These gifts are only a small portion of our true wealth, Great One, but we humbly offer them to you, praying that as you receive them, they may bring healing to others. Help us to follow the example of Christ and be willing to give more—all we have—that your name may be glorified. Amen.

Benediction
As you leave this place,
Remember the blessing that you have received.
While we were still sinners, Christ was willing to suffer and die.
We have no claim to this gift, yet Christ gave freely anyway.
Go in awe and wonder at the awesome one we serve.

Resurrection of the Lord

Scripture
Acts 10:34-43 *or Jeremiah 31:1-6*
Psalm 118:1-2, 14-24
Colossians 3:1-4 *or Acts 10:34-43*
John 20:1-18 *or Matthew 28:1-10*

Call to Worship
One: The Lord Jesus the Christ is risen!
Let us take up our tambourines and rejoice with dancing!
Many: The LORD has loved us with an everlasting love.
God has shown great faithfulness to the people.
One: The steadfast love of the LORD endures forever.
God is the God of all Israel and all nations.
Many: Our salvation has come to us in the resurrection.
Our Lord and savior has made a way for all people to be reconciled.
One: Let us come and praise God for God's love is wonderful.
Let us worship the LORD who has renewed our hope.
Many: Our salvation is in the LORD.
Thanks and praises be to God on high!

Invocation
As we worship you in this sanctuary, Redeeming God, we pray that you will find us faithful. Fill us with newness of life. Remind us of the wondrous gift given to us through your Son, Jesus the Christ. Restore our faith in you and in our hope of our own resurrection. Re-make us once again. Amen.

Call to Confession
We come before God with humility and in repentance, but we also come confessing our sins with great confidence in our redemption. We know that Jesus' work for humanity was sufficient for all our misdeeds. Let us confess those misdeeds before God, placing faith in God's promises to redeem.

Prayer of Confession
LORD, we are not worthy to call ourselves your children. We have

sinned by ignoring you and your command to love. We have allowed the things in this world to overcome our senses and to overwhelm our being in ways that have caused us to forget how to place you first in our lives. Hear our Prayer of Confession, and forgive us, we pray.

Assurance of Forgiveness
Although we are truly unworthy to call ourselves God's children, God has regarded us as heirs of the righteousness that only God can give. We have become heirs through the work of Jesus the Christ. It is through his work and the faith we have in Jesus that we are forgiven. Thanks be to God!

Offertory Invitation
No treasure can be exchanged for the salvation we have received from Jesus this day. No gift is worthy of the many gifts we have received through God's Spirit. In this time of offering, we humbly give back to God that which we can, praying that others may receive the same blessings from God through our offering that we have already received.

Offertory Prayer
Before you, O God, we have given of our treasure. In this time, we also offer our gifts of time and talents and any other gift that pleases you. We place our faith in you that all our gifts may be used so that your kingdom may come and your will may be done on earth. Amen.

Benediction
Christ is risen,
He is risen indeed!
Go therefore into all the world
making disciples and telling all about the good news of Christ's resurrection!
Amen.

Resurrection of the Lord Alternate

Scripture
Acts 10:34-43 *or Jeremiah 31:1-6*
Psalm 118:1-2, 14-24
Colossians 3:1-4 *or Acts 10:34-43*
John 20:1-18 *or Matthew 28:1-10*

Call to Worship
One: Christ the Lord is risen today!
Christ is risen, Hallelujah!
Many: We who have been risen with Christ
Shall seek the things that are above, where Christ is.
One: Christ reigns above forever and ever.
Christ now sits at the right hand of God.
Many: Therefore, we must not set our minds on things that are of this earth.
We must instead set our minds on things that are above.
One: We place our trust in Christ alone.
He is the one ordained by God to judge the living and the dead.
Many: Let everything that has breath praise the LORD!
In Christ, all things are made new!

Invocation
Glorious and wondrous God, we praise you today as we are reminded of the awesome work you did through Jesus the Christ for the sake of us, your people. Let your Spirit move through this place today, blowing deeply into our hearts and renewing the excitement, commitment, and faith we have in you and your coming kingdom! Amen.

Call to Confession
Setting aside our human pride, we come to God in this time offering our heartfelt repentance for the ways we have chosen to disobey God's will or ways that we have missed the mark set for us. God knows these things already, and we choose to confess them that we may be made clean once more.

Prayer of Confession
God of all, you know all our faults. You know all the ways that we have been unfaithful to you and to our fellow human beings. Remind us of these things and give us hearts of true repentance that we may seek forgiveness for ourselves and that we may make a truthful effort to go and sin no more.

Assurance of Forgiveness
The gift given to us through the victory won by Jesus is exactly what we have been praying for. We have the gift of forgiveness when we go to God, confessing our sins. We pray with the faith that God is willing and able through Christ to forgive all we have ever done. Go forth, praising God, for you have been made whole!

Offertory Invitation
What are we willing to give so that the kingdom of God can be made present in the world where we live? What are we willing to give to advance the name of Christ, the love of God, and the inspiration of the Holy Spirit? Let us give gratefully, prayerfully, and generously.

Offertory Prayer
Our offerings are here before you, Great God of all. May we dedicate them, along with our entire selves, to your work in the world. We pray that they would reach farther into the world than we can imagine, carrying your mercy and your love to all your people. Amen.

Benediction
The story of love has been completed in Jesus the Christ.
The world is redeemed.
May the blessings of our savior Jesus the Christ, the awesome love of God, and the inspiration given by the Holy Spirit be with you all, now and forever more. Amen.

Second Sunday of Easter

Scripture
Acts 2:14a, 22-32
Psalm 16
1 Peter 1:3-9
John 20:19-31

Call to Worship
One: Be with us, O LORD.
It is in you that we take our refuge.
Many: You are the LORD our God.
We have nothing good apart from you.
One: The LORD is our chosen portion and our cup.
We bless the LORD, who gives us wise counsel.
Many: In the day, the LORD is our instructor.
During the night, the LORD continues to teach us in our hearts.
One: We shall keep the LORD always before us and shall not be moved.
Our hearts shall be glad, and our souls shall rejoice in God.
Many: You have not given us up to Sheol nor let your faithful ones see the Pit.
You show us the paths of life, and in your presence, there is fullness of joy.

Invocation
We come into your presence this day praising you for the love you have shown to us through our Savior, Jesus the Christ. We bless you for the faithfulness you have shown to us as a loving parent. We give thanks for the continual presence of the Holy Spirit in our hearts and minds. Breathe into us in fresh and inspiring ways today and help us to become more like the people you have called us to be. Amen.

Call to Confession
We profess faith in Jesus the Christ, risen on Easter, who has come that we all may be freed from our sins and the power of death. Until we confess our sins, they remain ever with us. When we have confessed and repented, they are removed from us. Let us confess and repent together.

Prayer of Confession
Gracious and loving God, we have tried to hide our sins from you and from one another. We have rationalized the ways we have neglected the least of these, whom Jesus taught us to care for. We have often chosen the way of convenience instead of the way of love. Forgive us, we pray, and lead us forward in your eternal way.

Assurance of Forgiveness
God has not abandoned the souls of the faithful to Sheol. Instead, through Jesus the Christ, God has taken away our sins and has restored us to full righteousness. In Christ we are made new creations, freed from sin and freed from the fear of death! Thanks be to God!

Offertory Invitation
Although we have not seen Christ, we love him. One way that we can show our devotion to Jesus the Christ is through our time of offering. When we give to Christ's church, we give that we may proclaim the good news of the gospel and that we may minister to the least among us. Let us give generously.

Offertory Prayer
We place these gifts in your hands, Ruler of all, and along with these gifts, we place our lives. We pray that you would use them, that you would increase their effectiveness, and that you would help us to have hearts to dedicate ourselves and our gifts even more fully. Amen.

Benediction
Blessings to all who love the Lord!
We who have believed even though we have not seen are called blessed by Jesus.
Let us rejoice with indescribable and glorious joy.
Amen.

Third Sunday of Easter

Scripture
Acts 2:14a, 36-41
Psalm 116:1-4, 12-19
1 Peter 1:17-23
Luke 24:13-35

Call to Worship
One: Let us love the LORD, because God has heard our cries.
Because God's ear was inclined to us, let us call upon God as long as we live.
Many: What shall we return to the LORD for all God's bounty to us?
Let us lift up the cup of salvation and call upon God's name.
One: We pay our vows to the LORD in the presence of all God's people.
We are thankful to be called God's servants.
Many: O LORD, we are your servants. You have redeemed us.
We offer thanksgiving sacrifices and call upon your name.
One: Let us worship the LORD in truth and with great rejoicing.
God has called us into blessed relationship with God and one another.
Many: We will call upon the LORD all our days.
In the courts of the house of the LORD, we give our praises to God.

Invocation
In all days you have called your people, O LORD. We are grateful to be worshiping you together this day. Make yourself known to us. Re-invest your Spirit in us. Call us into greater service and help us to be energized to do your work in your world. May our praise be acceptable to you.

Call to Confession
When Peter spoke to the people and explained the good news of Jesus' gospel, they were cut to the heart because they had either not known the things that had been done or had misunderstood them. All of us in knowing and unknowing ways have participated

in the sins of this world. Let us confess together.

Prayer of Confession
Merciful God of all, we confess that we have sinned against you. We have not been the people you have called us to be. We have pursued things that do not satisfy, while you have continued to offer us things that will satisfy eternally. Forgive us and help us to be better.

Assurance of Forgiveness
The Lord Jesus offers forgiveness to all those who will repent. Repentance is not easy. It will cost us. Sometimes it will cost us things that are dear to us. But when we turn from our sin and honestly desire to keep ourselves free from that sin, Jesus is faithful to forgive. Thanks be to God.

Offertory Invitation
The Psalmist writes, "What shall I return to the LORD for all God's bounty to me?" There is no offering humans can give to equal the gifts we have been given by our God and creator. Let us strive to give as much of ourselves as we can, so that God may be proclaimed throughout the world.

Offertory Prayer
God above all, we bring our gifts to your church this day. Give us the strength we need to let go of our gifts and realize that they belong only to you. Help our fellowship to have the ability to use these gifts wisely that they would become a part of the healing of your world. Amen.

Benediction
Let the entire world know with certainty that God has made Jesus both Lord and Messiah,
The same Jesus who was crucified.
Proclaim Jesus, that the world may come to know and believe.
And may Jesus bless you abundantly as you go to do God's work.
Amen.

Fourth Sunday of Easter

Scripture
Acts 2:42-47
Psalm 23
1 Peter 2:19-25
John 10:1-10

Call to Worship
One: The LORD our God has called us together as sheep of one fold.
We hear Christ's voice, and we are led by Christ.
Many: We will not follow after strangers,
For we know the voice of our shepherd and master.
One: We come that we may hear the voice of the master.
We come to know what our shepherd would say to us.
Many: Let us hear the voice of Jesus.
Let us know and follow Christ's paths for our lives.
One: We shall celebrate the love Christ has for us and we have for the LORD.
We honor God with our worship this day.
Many: Let us enter into these gates with thanksgiving,
Giving all glory and honor to God the Creator, the Savior, and the Holy Spirit.

Invocation
Lord God, you have called us here and you have brought us to this time of worship. We humbly ask that you would respond with your Spirit in our hearts and minds during this time. Cause us to recognize you. Make your presence clear to us. Help us to respond to your presence with true, undistracted worship. Amen.

Call to Confession
We are all like sheep who have sometimes gone our own way. Even when Christ is calling us to his pastures, we have thought other pastures may be greener, and have strayed. This time of confession is an opportunity for us to repent of those sins and receive forgiveness.

Prayer of Confession
Holy and Awesome God, we confess that we have strayed from your paths. We have sometimes valued our own well-being more than your kingdom's well-being. We have placed ourselves above others and have forgotten that we are all your children, created in your image. Forgive us, we pray, and help us be better.

Assurance of Forgiveness
Our Lord and our Great Shepherd knows we are imperfect. It was because we are imperfect that Jesus was willing to come to the earth on our behalf. When we ask for forgiveness of our sins, and when we truly desire to put those sins behind us and be faithful to God, God is faithful to forgive.

Offertory Invitation
As people of God, we can easily recognize that we have received many more gifts than we have deserved from the hands of our generous and loving ruler. We come to this time in our worship with an opportunity to faithfully respond to those many, many gifts.

Offertory Prayer
In your mercy, LORD, receive these gifts offered to you and to your kingdom here on earth. We pray for their effectiveness in eliminating discord among your people, in healing the sick and wounded, in feeding the hungry, and in caring for the poor. May these be our goals, and may they be the great reach of these gifts. Amen.

Benediction
As we close our worship this day,
Go, seeking Christ who is the gate.
Go, inviting others to the gate we know in Christ.
Go, with the blessings of Almighty God, the Great Shepherd, and the faithful Spirit.
Amen.

Fifth Sunday of Easter

Scripture
Acts 7:55-60
Psalm 31:1-5, 15-16
1 Peter 2:2-10
John 14:1-14

Call to Worship
One: In you, O LORD, do we seek our refuge.
In your righteousness, LORD, deliver us and incline your ear to us.
Many: Rescue us speedily, O God. Be a rock of refuge for us.
Be to us, O LORD, a strong fortress of salvation.
One: You are indeed our rock and our fortress.
For the sake of your name, God, lead us and guide us.
Many: We commit our spirits into your hands, O LORD.
You have redeemed us, great and faithful God.
One: All our times are in your hands. Keep us from times of trouble.
Hear us when we call to you, and in your faithfulness, care for your people.
Many: Let your face shine upon us, for we are your servants.
Save us, your people, in your steadfast love.

Invocation
We come to you in great anticipation. We seek to find you here. We look to experience your Spirit within our hearts and minds. We yearn for your renewal of our spirits. Come, LORD God, be with us here, and re-create us in your image, making us wholly yours. Amen.

Call to Confession
When we are honest with ourselves, we can see our sinful nature. As humans we are prone to greed, we are prone to value ourselves more highly than those around us, and we are likely to rationalize the ways that we have strayed from the path God has placed before us. We are all in need of grace, that we may be redeemed. Let us confess before our God.

Prayer of Confession
Holy and Gracious God of all, we confess that we have sinned. In many ways we may recognize our sinfulness, and we ask for your gracious pardon. In other ways we may not even know we have missed your mark for us. Convict us of our misdeeds that we may repent and be healed.

Assurance of Forgiveness
Grace is a mysterious and wonderful gift, freely given to all those who turn their hearts and spirits toward God in repentance, trying to live in the way God has called them to live. We have confessed before God, and we have asked for grace and forgiveness. Know that in the name of Christ, we have been forgiven this day.

Offertory Invitation
Many in this world live in need. The mission of the church is to create disciples and to care for those who are in need throughout the globe. As a church, we realize that faithful discipleship includes giving of our resources that we may care for others near and far. Let us give generously in the name of Christ.

Offertory Prayer
Thank you, LORD of all, for the gracious gifts you have given to all of us. We are overwhelmed by the blessings you have given to us. Please receive these gifts we have given back to you this day. We pray that they may be used for your glory and for the healing of this world. Amen.

Benediction
Believe in God the creator,
Believe also in Jesus the Christ,
and in the Holy Spirit that is coexistent with the creator and the Son.
Go now, and do great things in the name of the Holy Trinity,
and may you receive blessing and honor in God's name.
Amen.

Sixth Sunday of Easter

Scripture
Acts 17:22-31
Psalm 66:8-20
1 Peter 3:13-22
John 14:15-21

Call to Worship
One: Bless our God, O peoples!
Let the sound of God's praise be heard!
Many: God has called us among the living,
God has kept our feet on solid ground.
One: Although God's people have been tested with fire and water,
God has brought us to a new and blessed place.
Many: We will come unto the LORD with offerings.
We will pay our vows to God.
One: Come and hear, all who fear the LORD.
Come as God's people share what God has done for them!
Many: Blessed be God for the LORD has given heed to our prayers.
God has kept steadfast love with us, God's people.

Invocation
LORD God, you have called us into relationship with you, one in which you have blessed us humans with the opportunity to learn of you and receive your love. We are overwhelmed by your blessings for us, and we gratefully acknowledge your steadfast love. Send your Spirit among us this day that we may once again be renewed in your presence.

Call to Confession
Jesus said that those who love Christ will keep his commandments. We are here proclaiming our love for Christ, but even with that love, we must confess that we have been unable to perfectly keep his commandments. Let us pray for forgiveness in this time of confession.

Prayer of Confession
Lord of all, your call on our lives is to be loving examples of your perfect love for your people. We have, in large and small ways, been unable to keep your commands fully. We have been unable to love you as you have loved your people. We have been unable to love others as ourselves. Please forgive us and help us to truly repent.

Assurance of Forgiveness
Jesus promised that we would not be orphaned, and the Holy Spirit continues to sustain and uphold us. Christ promised that those who love him and follow him would receive salvation. When we turn ourselves back to God, God has promised to receive us. People of God, we are forgiven.

Offertory Invitation
Often we have made idols of our things, of our wealth, and of many other things that are not God. We have even seemed to worship these things by pouring all we have into them instead of into the hands of our LORD. As we come to this time of offering, let us examine ourselves and place God above our worldly things.

Offertory Prayer
You are holy, LORD of all! We praise you for your faithfulness to us and to all people. These gifts are given in the sincere hope that they may be an acknowledgment of your sovereignty, and that they may be a blessing to your creation throughout the world. Amen.

Benediction
May the Lord of all,
the Creator, Savior, and Holy Spirit,
be with you all as you go into the world
Loving and caring for God and one another.
Amen.

Seventh Sunday of Easter

Scripture
Acts 1:6-14
Psalm 68:1-10, 32-35
1 Peter 4:12-14; 5:6-11
John 17:1-11

Call to Worship
One: Let the righteous be joyful; let them exult before God!
Let them be jubilant with joy!
Many: Sing to God, sing praises to God's name!
Lift up a song to the one who rides upon the clouds!
One: For that one is the LORD, the God of all creation!
Let us be exultant before our God.
Many: Sing to God, O kingdoms of the earth.
Sing praises to the LORD!
One: Ascribe to God power, for God's majesty is over the earth.
Give God glory, for God's power is from everlasting to everlasting.
Many: Awesome is our God before the nations.
God gives strength and power to God's people.

Invocation
Jesus said that he had made you known to those whom you had given to Jesus. LORD, make yourself known to us again this day. Let us recognize you in our songs, in our prayers, in the word, in the silences, in the music, and in all ways we encounter you in this time of worship. And as we meet you, make us more fully yours. Amen.

Call to Confession
We have been given the opportunity to come to God in humility, owning our misdeeds and mistakes, and letting them go. We have been called to do just that, so that we might be forgiven and so that we might be a more righteous people. Let us confess our sins before God.

Prayer of Confession
LORD of all, we confess that we have sinned against you and against your people. We have forgotten your ways. We have chosen paths that benefit us and limit your role in our lives. We have made choices that deny the importance of the people in our lives and all your children around the globe. We ask for forgiveness and for the will and ability to be more like Jesus.

Assurance of Forgiveness
The promise is sure--God has promised to forgive those who come and let go of their pride, asking for forgiveness and asking for God's help. The One who made that promise is certain in faithfulness. Because we have repented, we have been forgiven. We give thanks to God for this assurance.

Offertory Invitation
Peter wrote of discipline. One of the hardest things about our time of offering is having the discipline to give as we ought. Giving takes faith, certainly, but it also takes the discipline to do what our faith is telling us we must. Let us give as we have been called.

Offertory Prayer
God of all, Great and Mighty One, bless these gifts that we have given today. Use them for your glory and for the care of your people throughout the globe. Cause us to be a part of your plan of redemption for the world through these gifts of our treasure and through the gift of our service. Amen.

Benediction
As Jesus prayed that God would glorify him,
let us go into the world,
doing all we can to glorify the Lord of all the earth,
Jesus the Christ.
And may all God's blessings go with every one of us.
Amen.

Ascension of the Lord

Scripture
Acts 1:1-11
Psalm 47 *or Psalm 93*
Ephesians 1:15-23
Luke 24:44-53

Call to Worship
One: Clap your hands, all you peoples;
Shout to God with loud songs of joy!
Many: For the LORD, the most high, is awesome.
God is the great king over all the earth.
One: Sing praises to God, sing praises!
God has gone up with a shout, the LORD with the sound of a trumpet!
Many: Sing praises to our ruler, the one and only God!
For God is the king over all the earth.
One: God is king over all nations;
God sits on the holiest of thrones.
Many: Sing, clap, shout to the LORD our God,
For God is great and is greatly to be praised!

Invocation
LORD of all, you are great indeed. Your glory reaches into all places in the universe. Let your glory and wonder reach into this worship space, changing this place from an earthly space to a holy and heavenly one. Transform our world, transform our sanctuary and transform our hearts by your wonderful presence here. Amen.

Call to Confession
We who love the Lord are called to remember the ways that we have sinned. God has promised to forgive our sins when we openly and honestly confess them and humble ourselves before God in repentance. Let us offer our words of confession together.

Prayer of Confession
God, you are holy. There is no shadow of iniquity in you. You

know our thoughts, our deeds, and all our ways. We confess that we have been unable to live perfectly according to your standards. We have sinned by not loving our sisters and brothers. We have sinned by placing idols in our lives in the place you should hold alone. Forgive us and give us the strength to truly repent.

Assurance of Forgiveness
As Jesus was about to ascend to the heavens, he reminded the disciples that the Christ was sent into the world for the forgiveness of sins. Those who turn to God, confessing their sins and choosing to repent have already been forgiven in the name of Jesus the Christ. Thanks be to God!

Offertory Invitation
God is ruler over all things, all principalities, all nations, and all people. All we have ultimately belongs to God. God has called us to use those gifts given by God to be the body of Christ in the world. Let us give that we may heal, comfort, and care for all in need.

Offertory Prayer
We give thanks, gracious God, for the gifts you have given to us, and we ask for your blessing on these gifts we have returned to you. Please help your servants to use all we have and all we can be to be blessings to your people wherever they are. Amen.

Benediction
Let us go, with our eyes enlightened,
that we may proclaim the risen Savior in every way we can,
in every place we can, with all the means we can.
Go with the blessings of a wonderful God.
Amen.

Day of Pentecost

Scripture
Acts 2:1-21 *or Numbers 11:24-30*
Psalm 104:24-34, 35b
1 Corinthians 12:3b-13 *or Acts 2:1-21*
John 20:19-23 *or John 7:37-39*

Call to Worship
One: The Spirit of the LORD has come!
The Spirit of God touches the people like burning fire.
Many: May the fire of your Spirit ignite our hearts, O God.
May we be changed by encountering your glory.
One: God proclaimed through the prophet Joel, and God continues to proclaim:
God's Spirit will be poured out on all flesh, all people shall see it.
Many: Let your Spirit be poured out on your people this day, God of all.
Let us know the wonderful presence of your Holy Spirit.
One: God has come among us, here in this place.
God meets us, even as we come to worship the LORD.
Many: May the fire of your Spirit ignite our hearts, O God!
May we be changed by encountering your glory!

Invocation
Come, LORD God, come. Enter into this sanctuary. Send your Spirit into every heart, every mind, every person gathered here. May our worship be true, our change be real, and our newness be lasting. Come, LORD God, and give us your Spirit again that we may do wondrous deeds in your name. Amen.

Call to Confession
We all share the need for forgiveness with every other human. No one is able to live a life of perfection. As hard as we may try, we are unable to avoid every possible sin. Jesus has promised that when we confess those sins and ask for forgiveness, he will be faithful to forgive. We confess with confidence in the grace of Jesus.

Prayer of Confession
Everlasting One, we confess that we have lived sinful lives. As individuals and as communities we have been unable to learn how to live lives of love toward you and toward our neighbors. We have forgotten the needs of many in pursuit of our own satisfaction. Please forgive us and give us new hearts for serving you and your people.

Assurance of Forgiveness
In confessing, we have been forgiven. In turning from our sinfulness and determining to do better with the help of God, we can be better disciples of the Lord Jesus, the Christ. Let us celebrate our forgiveness and work toward a better future of service.

Offertory Invitation
We have all been given many gifts. **Scripture** affirms this, and we know it to be true when we look at our lives. We are called to give those gifts to God that they may be a blessing for the entire community of believers, and for all humanity. Let us give of all our gifts that the world may be healed.

Offertory Prayer
Light of the world, we have given back to you a portion of the gifts of treasure with which you have blessed us. We pray that all our gifts may also be returned to you, gifts of service, labor and many others that all your people may receive your blessings. Bless our giving and renew our desire to give more. Amen.

Benediction
Jesus said to his disciples, "Peace be with you. Even as God sent me, so I am sending you."
As Jesus' disciples, we must remember we are always being sent into the world to give Christ's gifts.
Let us go, sharing the blessings we have received with all those we meet.
Amen.

Trinity Sunday

Scripture
Genesis 1:1-2:4a
Psalm 8
2 Corinthians 13:11-13
Matthew 28:16-20

Call to Worship
One: God is glorified in all creation.
Our God is beauty beyond all measure.
Many: The LORD spoke, and the worlds were created.
Through the word of God, all things came to be.
One: Christ was present at creation and was made flesh in Jesus.
Through the Christ, we have the assurance of salvation.
Many: Jesus was fully God and fully human.
His work was the redemption of all the world.
One: The Spirit came at Pentecost and was given to all Christ's disciples.
Through the Spirit, all creation has its life and breath.
Many: The Spirit continues to sustain and empower all who call upon the LORD.
Thanks be to God, the great Trinity!

Invocation
Great maker of all things, we worship you for your gift of creation. We praise you for the gift of life and the opportunity we have to serve you, the one, true God. Visit us here in this place, during these moments of worship. Renew your Spirit within us and cause us to be wholly yours. Amen.

Call to Confession
When God created the heavens and the earth, God proclaimed that all that had been made was good. While God's work was perfect, humanity is not perfect. We have failed to uphold the goodness with which we were created in God's image. Let us confess our sinfulness before God together.

Prayer of Confession
LORD, you are perfect. You created us to be people who uphold your law and who follow your will. We have been unable to do this perfectly. Instead, we have placed ourselves in the center of our lives instead of you. Help us to re-order our lives and minds that we may truly repent and may live lives that honor you.

Assurance of Forgiveness
The second person of the Trinity, Christ, incarnate in Jesus of Nazareth, taught us that our faith in Christ and our willingness to repent are at the source of our salvation. When we truly repent and trust in Christ for our salvation, we will be forgiven of our sins. Thanks be to God!

Offertory Invitation
In this time of worship, we turn ourselves toward worship of God by giving to the work God has for the world and for the church. Let us search our hearts and minds and let us give generously to the church and to the kingdom of God that all people may know the good news, and all may have their needs fulfilled.

Offertory Prayer
Thank you, LORD, for giving us hearts of generosity. Thank you for the gifts you have given to us that we may give back to you. We give in love for you and for your people, praying that these gifts may reach far and wide to bring glory to your name and your kingdom on earth. Amen.

Benediction
Always remember to greet one another in love,
And may the grace of the Lord Jesus Christ, the love of God, and the communion of the Holy Spirit be with all of you, now and forever. Amen.

Proper 3

Scripture
Isaiah 49:8-16a
Psalm 131
1 Corinthians 4:1-5
Matthew 6:24-34

Call to Worship
One: O LORD, our hearts are not lifted up,
Our eyes are not raised too high.
Many: We do not occupy ourselves with things too great.
We do not worry over things too marvelous for us.
One: Instead, we have calmed and quieted our souls.
We have made ourselves like the weaned child with its mother.
Many: We give the things of our hearts over to you,
Just as a child relies on its mother for all it needs.
One: LORD God, you are our hope forever more.
You are the fortress upon which our lives are built.
Many: We love and adore you more than any other.
Always allow our hope to be in you alone.

Invocation
God, you have inscribed us in the palm of your hand. We are yours. We look to you for our guidance, we look to you for our fulfillment, and we praise you for your overwhelming presence in our lives and in your world. Send your Spirit among us, that we may be utterly amazed by you once more. Amen.

Call to Confession
Even when we are not aware of anything that may be against us, it is not we who judge ourselves, but the LORD who judges all. We therefore turn to God in repentance for misdeeds known and unknown to us. Let us confess our sins before our God.

Prayer of Confession
Great and Holy Master, we confess that we have not been the faithful people you have called us to be. We have allowed our humanity to rule our hearts rather than Christ's divinity. We pray

for your forgiveness, and that you would renew within us the new hearts and new Spirits given to all those who are found in Christ Jesus.

Assurance of Forgiveness
We should break forth into song, and we should sing with great exultation, because the LORD has comforted us, God's people. God chooses in great grace and mercy to have compassion on us. When we confess before God, we are redeemed. Praise be to the God of all things!

Offertory Invitation
No one can serve two masters. Either they will hate the one and love the other or be devoted to one and despise the other. You cannot serve both God and wealth. Let us give as people who serve God alone.

Offertory Prayer
May these blessings be acceptable to you, Mighty God. May they be a source of strength for many, may they be a sign of true dependence upon you, and may they be used wholly for the spread of your love throughout all the world. Amen.

Benediction
As you go from this place of worship today, remember these words from our Savior:
Seek first the kingdom of God, and God's righteousness,
and all the things you seek and worry about will be added to you as well.
Amen.

Proper 4

Scripture
Genesis 6:9-22; 7:24, 8:14-19 *or Deuteronomy 11:18-21, 26-28*
Psalm 46 *or Psalm 31:1-5, 19-24*
Romans 1:16-17; 3:22b-28 (29-31)
Matthew 7:21-29

Call to Worship
One: God is our refuge and our strength,
A very present help in trouble.
Many: Therefore, we will not fear, even though the earth should change.
We will not fear even though the mountains shake in the heart of the sea.
One: There is a river whose streams make glad the city of God,
The holy habitation of the Most High.
Many: God is in the midst of the city, it shall not be moved.
God will help it when the morning dawns.
One: "Be still and know that I am God," says the LORD.
"I am exalted among the nations, I am exalted in the earth."
Many: The LORD of hosts is with us;
The God of Jacob is our refuge.

Invocation
Meet us here, Great God above all. Enter our worship space. Rush in like the winds of Pentecost. Fill our hearts, fill our minds, fill our bodies and souls with you alone. As we worship, make us to know that we have met with the one true God, the great master of the cosmos, and change us to be more like the people you have called us to be. Amen.

Call to Confession
Paul writes that all have sinned and fallen short of the glory of God. There is no distinction of righteous and unrighteous, because all are sinners in need of God's grace. Let us confess to God the ways we have sinned, that we may be made whole once again.

Prayer of Confession
Great giver of grace, we confess that we have fallen short of your glory. We have not loved you as we ought. We have not loved our neighbors as ourselves. In every way that we have sinned, God, we are heartily sorry, and we ask that you would once again forgive us and lead us forward in renewed relationship with you.

Assurance of Forgiveness
Paul continues that although all have sinned and fallen short of the glory of God, we are now justified through our faith in God which is a gift to all who seek redemption through Christ Jesus. In the faithful act of confession, God has extended forgiveness to us, God's people. Thanks be to God!

Offertory Invitation
Our faithfulness to God is shown in many ways. In our actions, in our words, in our meditations, we show our faithfulness to God. The giving of our treasures for God's glory is another act of faithfulness to our God. Let us give generously and faithfully.

Offertory Prayer
Holy God, we ask that you would accept these gifts to you. May we have the wisdom to use them as you would have us use them. May we have the discipline and dedication to give to you as we ought. May these gifts be used to reach in love to all your people wherever they may be found. Amen.

Benediction
May the Lord bless you and keep you,
May the Lord's countenance be upon you,
May the Lord lift you up and give you the peace that comes only from God.
Amen.

Proper 5

Scripture
Genesis 12:1-9 *or Hosea 5:15-6:6*
Psalm 33:1-12 *or Psalm 50:7-15*
Romans 4:13-25
Matthew 9:9-13, 18-26

Call to Worship
One: Rejoice in the LORD, O you righteous! Praise befits the upright.
Praise the LORD with the lyre, make melody to God with the harp.
Many: Sing to God a new song, play skillfully on the strings, with loud shouts.
For the word of the LORD is upright, and all God's work is done in faithfulness.
One: God loves righteousness and justice;
The earth is full of the steadfast love of the LORD.
Many: By the word of the LORD, the heavens were made.
All the heavenly host were created by the breath of God's mouth.
One: The counsel of the LORD stands forever,
The thoughts of God's heart last from generation to generation.
Many: Happy are the people whose God is the LORD,
The people whom the LORD has chosen for a heritage.

Invocation
LORD God, creator of all, you have taken us, your people, to be your constant companion. You have loved the church as spouses love one another. Come again to us this day. Enter into our hearts and minds, and give us the same affection for you that you have for us. Let us live as a community wedded to you, the one true God. Amen.

Call to Confession
As Jesus called the disciples, he simply said to them, "Come, follow me." The disciples of that day got up, left what they were doing, and followed Jesus. We, too, are to get up, leave whatever else we are doing, and follow Jesus. Sometimes we have done this

well, other times, we have not. Let us confess before our God.

Prayer of Confession
Gracious One, we confess that even when we have the best intentions to follow in the footsteps of your son, Jesus, the Christ, we are unable to do so perfectly. We cannot live up to the standard set by Christ. Yet we trust in your mercy, knowing that in Christ we can be forgiven. Please forgive us once more and cause us to know true repentance.

Assurance of Forgiveness
The grace of God is offered to all those who believe in the salvation God offers. Through faith, God offers righteousness. This has been the promise since the time of Abraham, and in Christ, that promise was renewed to all people in all nations. Let us rejoice in this promise of forgiveness!

Offertory Invitation
God desires mercy not sacrifice. Giving of our treasures is a blessing to us and a blessing to God only when we give out of love for God and our neighbor. We therefore do not give out of obligation, but in the desire that all people may know relationship with God. Let us give generously and lovingly.

Offertory Prayer
LORD God, master of the universe, you have all things at your command. You have given us the opportunity to worship you in this time of offering by allowing us to have treasures we can dedicate back to you. Please take all these gifts. Use them and use us to your glory. Amen.

Benediction
As this worship service ends,
A new calling begins.
Jesus continues to invite us to be faithful.
Christ stands at the door of our hearts and says, "Come, follow me."
Let us be found faithfully following Christ our Lord.
Amen.

Proper 6

Scripture
Genesis 18:1-15, (21:1-7) or Exodus 19:2-8a
Psalm 116:1-2, 12-19 or Psalm 100
Romans 5:1-8
Matthew 9:35-10:8, (9-23)

Call to Worship
One: Love the LORD, because the LORD hears your voice.
Love the LORD your God, because God listens to your supplications.
Many: The LORD has inclined an ear to us.
We will call upon the LORD as long as we live.
One: Let us lift up the cup of salvation and call on the name of the LORD.
Let us pay our vows to God in the presence of all people.
Many: O LORD, we are your servants.
We worship you, for you have loosened our bonds.
One: Offer a thanksgiving sacrifice to God.
Call upon the name of the LORD.
Many: We profess faith in the LORD our God.
In all times and all places we will praise the LORD!

Invocation
LORD God, you have proved yourself over and over to be true to your promises. You have promised that where people are gathered together in your name, you will be there. We call upon you now, so that you will join us as we worship you. Stir within our hearts faithfulness, praise, and wonder at you. Amen.

Call to Confession
God proves God's love for us in that while we were still sinners Christ died for us. Through Christ we have inherited the opportunity to call God our parent. In humility, we come to God now, confessing ways that we have not lived up to that name in our lives. Let us confess together.

Prayer of Confession
Awesome God, you have been our rock and our shield in all times. We confess now that we have often strayed from the way you set before us. We have not been faithful to our promises or to the covenant you established with your people. Forgive our sins, and continually make us better.

Assurance of Forgiveness
While we were still sinners, Christ came to take away our sin. We cannot do enough to earn that redemption. It is only offered to us through grace. When we come before God, humbly asking for God's forgiveness for our sins, God will always be faithful to forgive. Thanks to God for this great assurance!

Offertory Invitation
Jesus sent his disciples out into all the countryside of Israel to take his message forward. They traveled together, preaching Christ's redemptive word. We are privileged to participate in Christ's work in the world by spreading the word through our actions and through our gifts. Let us give generously.

Offertory Prayer
Please accept these gifts that we bring before you this day, holy God. We pray that they will bless your people and they will show your love to all the world within our reach. Please bless us that we may be guided by your Spirit to use these gifts and to give of ourselves more fully. Amen.

Benediction
The harvest is plentiful, but the laborers are few.
As one body of Christ, let us go into the world,
laboring for the great harvest of Jesus the Christ.
Amen.

Proper 7

Scripture
Genesis 21:8-21 *or Jeremiah 20:7-13*
Psalm 86:1-10, 16-17 *or Psalm 69:7-10, (1-15), 16-18*
Romans 6:1b-11
Matthew 10:24-39

Call to Worship
One: Incline your ear to me, O LORD, and answer me.
I am poor and needy, but I am devoted to you.
Many: Save your servants who trust in you O LORD.
Be gracious to us, for you are our God.
One: Gladden the soul of your servant,
For to you, O LORD, I lift up my soul.
Many: Give ear, O God, to our supplication.
In days of trouble we will call upon you, for you will answer.
One: There is none like you, Mighty and Holy One.
Nowhere is there anything that compares to your works.
Many: For you are great and do wondrous things; you alone are God.
Turn to us and be gracious to us.

Invocation
LORD God, your faithfulness to your people is overwhelming. Your love is gracious and wonderful beyond measure. We worship you here, and we long to hear your voice, see your face, and feel your touch. Restore in us passion for your desires. Cause us to become greater workers for your kingdom throughout the world. Instill in us the excitement of working for you. Amen.

Call to Confession
We do not sin more so that our grace in Christ can increase. Instead, we do all we can to live our lives with as few sins as possible, knowing that this honors our God. When we have sinned, we are invited to turn to God and ask for forgiveness. Let us pray together as one.

Prayer of Confession
Creator of all, we confess that we have sinned against you and against your creation. We have not cared for one another but have used one another to our benefit. We have not placed you first in our lives but have instead placed our own wants and desires ahead of pleasing you. Forgive us, we pray. Help us to better serve you and draw us into deeper relationship.

Assurance of Forgiveness
Those who have chosen Christ have crucified our old selves and have invited our new selves, the ones ruled by our Lord, to enter in. Through our confession, we have renewed our desire to be one with Christ. All who have died to our old selves have been freed from our sins. Thanks to God for this amazing grace!

Offertory Invitation
Jesus says that it is enough for the disciple to be like the teacher. We, who are disciples of Christ, work to be more like our model. Christ was willing to give all for the sake of others. What are we willing to give for the kingdom of God?

Offertory Prayer
In your mercy, Lord, receive these blessings. They are only a portion of the blessings we have received from you, but we pray that they may be, in your hands, healing in your world and love to your people. May we be willing to give as Christ gave that the world may be what you desire. Amen.

Benediction
Let us go, taking up our crosses, proclaiming the good news from the mountaintops,
And let us receive God's blessings as we serve the great Trinity. Creator, Savior, and Holy Spirit!

Proper 8

Scripture
Genesis 22:1-14 *or Jeremiah 28:5-9*
Psalm 13 *or Psalm 89:1-4, 15-18*
Romans 6:12-23
Matthew 10:40-42

Call to Worship
One: The LORD is our faithful guide and companion.
God is with us through all our days.
Many: Though storms may come, though trials arise,
God's love stands with us in all times and places.
One: God hears us as we cry out.
Lift up your voices to the LORD and await God's answer.
Many: Consider us and answer us, LORD of all!
Give light to our eyes, speak your message to our hearts.
One: Let us trust in the steadfast love of the LORD.
Our hearts shall rejoice in the salvation of God.
Many: We will sing to the LORD because God has dealt bountifully with us.
We will praise God with all we have.

Invocation
Great and Gracious God, you show mercy to us all. You showed mercy to your servant Abraham long ago and you have continued to deal with your people in love and mercy throughout the ages. Give us eyes to see and ears to hear your message to us this day. May our spirits be made one with yours. Amen.

Call to Confession
The Apostle Paul reminds us that when sin reigns over us, we are consumed with our worldly passions. All of us have lived in this way in some portion of our lives. All of us have been and are sinners. We confess together that God may forgive those sins and renew our wholeness in Christ.

Prayer of Confession
LORD, you alone are the holy one. You alone are perfect. We

come before you now, humbly confessing our sins. We have not loved you as we ought. We have forgotten your promises and your commands in our pursuit of things that satisfy. Forgive us, we pray, and make us yours again.

Assurance of Forgiveness
Now that we have been set free from our sins, let us live in service to righteousness. God has forgiven us of the sins that we have committed, both as individuals and as communities. Let us work now for the righteousness that comes with living as children of the light.

Offertory Invitation
One of the great joys of being a member of a community of worshipers is the opportunity we have to bring our resources together for the good of this community and the world. We give because we love to serve others. We give because we love Christ's church. We give, that the world may become what God has designed it to be.

Offertory Prayer
LORD, grant that these gifts given this day may become sacrifices for you. We pray that these sacrifices may be acceptable to you, and that they may be used in ways that will build your kingdom here on earth and will heal your people. Let us dedicate all we can to these efforts. Amen.

Benediction
Our blessing is this:
Now that we have been freed through Christ from sinfulness,
and now that we have truly become servants of God,
We are now blessed with sanctification.
May God continually renew that blessing for all of us.
Amen.

Proper 9

Scripture
Genesis 24:34-38, 42-49, 58-67 *or Zechariah 9:9-12*
Psalm 45:10-17 *or Psalm 145:8-14*
Romans 7:15-25a
Matthew 11:16-19, 25-30

Call to Worship
One: The LORD is gracious and merciful;
The LORD is slow to anger and abounding in steadfast love!
Many: The LORD is good to all.
God's compassion is over all that God has made.
One: All your works shall give thanks to you, O LORD.
All your faithful shall rise up and bless you.
Many: They shall speak of the glory of your kingdom.
They shall tell of your power.
One: They shall make known to all people your mighty deeds;
They shall tell of the glorious splendor of your kingdom.
Many: Your kingdom is everlasting, and you are faithful in all things.
The LORD upholds those who are falling and raises all who are bowed down.

Invocation
Your Holy Spirit, O LORD, fills this place. Your wind blows through our hearts, through our minds, and through our souls. Create within us a wonder, an awe, an excitement in all your works. Draw us to you that we can praise you more fully and love you completely. Amen.

Call to Confession
We do not even understand our own actions, we try to do what is right, but often it is our human nature that overwhelms, causing us to choose the precise thing we do not want to do. We need to ask for forgiveness for these missteps. Let us confess to God.

Prayer of Confession
Gracious One, we confess that we have often chosen the wrong

way. We have not followed after you. We have instead gratified ourselves through our humanity. Please forgive the wrong we have done and the poor choices we have made. Help us to choose your way, and yours alone.

Assurance of Forgiveness
Who will rescue us from this sinfulness? Who will rescue us from what Paul calls this "body of death?" Thanks be to God through Jesus Christ our Lord! Through Jesus, we who confess our sins are forgiven. Let us rejoice before our God!

Offertory Invitation
We have declared ourselves to be faithful followers of God. We are responsible as followers of God for gifts and sacrifices that will benefit this community and will take comforts to those in need throughout the world. The Lord needs our gifts, so that we can do all we can to work for God on earth. Let us give generously.

Offertory Prayer
Holy Trinity, we lift these gifts before you, asking that you would accept them and bless them. May they bring your word to the lost, your comfort to those who mourn, your healing to those who are sick and suffer, your release to those who are captive. May we dedicate these and all our gifts to you this day and every day.
Amen.

Benediction
Receive this blessing in the words of Christ our Lord:
Come to Christ, all who are weary and carrying heavy burdens,
And Christ will give you rest.
For Christ's yoke is easy and Christ's burden is light.
Thanks be to God!
Amen.

Proper 10

Scripture
Genesis 25:19-34 *or Isaiah 55:10-13*
Psalm 119:105-112 *or Psalm 65:(1-8), 9-13*
Romans 8:1-11
Matthew 13:1-9, 18-23

Call to Worship
One: Your word, O God, is a lamp to my feet.
Your word, O God, is a light to my path.
Many: We have sworn an oath and we have confirmed it.
Our covenant is to observe your righteous ordinances.
One: In our affliction, O LORD, give us life.
Accept our offerings of praise and teach us your ordinances.
Many: You are the LORD, our God,
We do not forget your law.
One: Even though a snare is laid for us,
We do not stray from your precepts.
Many: Your decrees are the joy of our hearts.
We incline our hearts to perform your statutes forever.

Invocation
In awe and wonder we come before you, gracious and merciful God. We are amazed at your power, but we are even more amazed at your love for us, your people. Reinvigorate us with your presence here this day. Let your Spirit fill us deeply and make us yours to our core. Amen.

Call to Confession
Paul writes that the mind that is set on the flesh is hostile to God. Even though we do our best to live in God's Spirit, we often succumb to our flesh, and this causes us to sin. Let us turn our thoughts to confession and let us ask for God's forgiveness.

Prayer of Confession
God over all creation, we come before you today confessing our sins and asking for your grace and mercy. In ways that we recall and in ways that we may not even be aware of, we have sinned

against you and your people. Please forgive any ways that we have strayed from your paths for us and help us to walk forward in your everlasting way.

Assurance of Forgiveness
Paul also writes that there is now no condemnation for those who are in Christ Jesus, for the law of the Spirit of Life in Christ Jesus has set us free from the law of sin and death. Those who are in Jesus are forgiven from their sins whenever they confess. Great is the grace of God!

Offertory Invitation
The love of God in Christ extends to the entire world. As the body of Christ, we are to be looking not only to the needs of our own community but outward to the needs of all God's children. Let us give generously that people all over the world can receive the blessings and the good news of Christ.

Offertory Prayer
God, we offer these gifts to you and we ask that they may be a blessing to you and to all your people wherever they may be found in the world. Let your love flow upon all people, and let this community be a part of your gifts of love to all the earth. Amen.

Benediction
Let us go forth,
as those of good soil,
letting the word of God be planted deeply within us,
growing strong roots,
and creating great fruit for God's kingdom.
Amen.

Proper 11

Scripture
Genesis 28:10-19a *or Isaiah 44:6-8*
Psalm 139:1-12, 23-24 *or Psalm 86:11-17*
Romans 8:12-25
Matthew 13:24-30, 36-43

Call to Worship
One: O LORD, you have searched us and known us.
You know when we sit down and when we rise up;
Many: You discern our thoughts from far away.
You search out our path and our lying down and are acquainted with all our ways.
One: Even before a word is on our tongues, O LORD, you know it completely.
You hem us in, behind and before, and lay your hand upon us.
Many: Such knowledge is too wonderful for us; It is so high we cannot attain it.
If we ascend to heaven, you are there; if we make our beds in Sheol, you are there.
One: If we take the wings of the morning and settle at the farthest limits of the sea,
Even there, your hand shall lead us, and your right hand shall hold us fast.
Many: If we say, "Surely the darkness shall cover us, and the light become night."
Even the darkness is not dark to you; the night is as bright as day.
All: Search us, O God, and know our hearts; test us and know our thoughts.
See if there is any wicked way in us and lead us in the way everlasting.

Invocation
In the place where Jacob saw a vision of a ladder going into the heavens, he had a wondrous encounter with you, Great LORD. In that moment, the heavens and earth met in Jacob's sight. We pray that our sanctuary may be such a place where heaven and earth may come together, and we may also have a wondrous encounter with you, here and now. Amen.

Call to Confession
Our time of confession is an opportunity. It is a chance for us to recognize our sin and the sins of our society, and to turn to God asking both for forgiveness and for strength to resist the temptations of our lives. Let us faithfully turn to God in confession.

Prayer of Confession
We thank you, God for your wonderful grace that gives us the chance of redemption. We offer our heartfelt repentance for any sinful ways within us. Forgive what we have done and what we have left undone. Through the gift given to us through Jesus, cleanse us from all sin, and lead us in your way everlasting.

Assurance of Forgiveness
When we receive the spirit of adoption, given to us through Christ, we become not only children of God, but heirs of all that God has to give. Foremost in the gifts God offers is the redemption of those who have faith in God and who love God. God has removed our sins from us. Let us walk forward in the light.

Offertory Invitation
Giving of our gifts to the church for the benefit of others is a joy to the believer. Together we can make substantial differences in the world in which we live. We can care for the sick, feed the hungry, and proclaim release of the captives. Let us give together that God's will may be done in God's world.

Offertory Prayer
Holy One, we pray that you will accept these gifts, gifts given in gratitude for all you have done for us and gifts given to proclaim your love throughout the world. Help us to use all we have and all we are to lift up the name of the Triune God, now and forever. Amen.

Benediction
As a united body of Christ, One in name and one in purpose,
Let us go forth from this place, Blessed by God the creator,
God the Savior, And God the Spirit, With the great hope of what we cannot yet see. Amen.

Proper 12

Scripture
Genesis 29:15-28 *or 1 Kings 3:5-12*
Psalm 105:1-11 *or Psalm 128 or Psalm 119:129-136*
Romans 8:26-39
Matthew 13:31-33, 44-52

Call to Worship
One: O give thanks to the LORD, call upon God's name,
Make known God's deeds among the peoples!
Many: Sing to God, sing praises to the LORD;
Tell of all God's wonderful works!
One: Glory in God's holy name;
let the hearts of those who seek the LORD rejoice!
Many: Seek the LORD and God's strength;
seek God's presence continually.
One: Remember the wonderful works God has done,
Remember God's miracles and the judgments God has uttered.
Many: For the LORD is our God; God's judgments are in all the earth.
God is mindful of the covenant forever! Thanks be to God!

Invocation
As we are reminded of your great and wondrous deeds in all the world, Great God, we come before you with a spirit of praise. As we enter into this time of worship, we invoke your Spirit to be among us. Let the winds of your Spirit flow within this space, filling us with wonder, with love, and with excitement to worship you. Amen.

Call to Confession
Confession is not an easy part of our walk with God, but it is a necessary one. Confessing means that we have to come to terms with the ways that we have erred in our lives. We have to remember those mistakes we have made, claim them as mistakes, and then ask for forgiveness. It is hard, but as believers, it is something we are called to do that we may be healed.

Prayer of Confession
We are fortunate to have a loving and forgiving God like you, O LORD. We turn to you in these moments, sorry for the ways that we have sinned in our lives. We have turned from your way. We have hurt our neighbors and ourselves. Please forgive our sins and help us to walk in your light. Amen.

Assurance of Forgiveness
Nothing separates us from God in Christ. Whatever we have done, wherever we have been, however we have lived, we are assured that when we confess those misdeeds to God and repent of our sinful ways, God will forgive. We give our thanks to God for that wonderful promise.

Offertory Invitation
The gifts that we have been given by God are not intended to be kept or hoarded by us. Instead, we are to live in community with one another and with all others, giving of the gifts we have received so that all people may have enough. Our offerings are one way to give in order to heal God's world. Let us give faithfully.

Offertory Prayer
Holy One, we lay our gifts before you. You alone can use them in the best possible way. We ask that you would receive these gifts and use them for your purposes in the world. May we always be willing to give, that others may hear the good news we have to share.

Benediction
Go with this blessing:
Nothing can separate us from God in Christ Jesus our Lord,
Not death, life, angels, rulers, things present, things to come, powers, height, depth, or anything else in all creation.
Let us rejoice in these promises forever!
Amen.

Proper 13

Scripture
Genesis 32:22-31 *or Isaiah 55:1-5*
Psalm 17: 1-7, 15 *or Psalm 145:8-9, 14-21*
Romans 9:1-5
Matthew 14:13-21

Call to Worship
One: Hear a just cause, O LORD; attend to my cry.
Give ear to my prayer, for my lips are free from deceit.
Many: From you, let my vindication come.
From you, O LORD, may I find salvation.
One: Try me, O LORD, visit me at night and test me.
I pray that you may find no wickedness within me.
Many: As for what others do, God,
By the word of your lips, I have avoided the ways of the violent.
One: My steps hold fast to your path. I call upon you,
For I know you will answer me. Incline your ear, O God, and hear my words.
Many: Wondrously show your steadfast love, O Savior of those who seek refuge!
I shall behold your face in righteousness. I adore and praise you!

Invocation
God of all times and places, we are here to worship you and to worship you alone. Our hearts and minds are sometimes far from you, in other places, worried about all kinds of things. Send your Spirit that we may focus our worship. Send your Spirit that we may be empowered for worship. Send your Spirit that we may meet you and be changed in wonderful ways this day. Amen.

Call to Confession
We often are able to look around us and see the ways that the world is sinful, or even the ways that other individuals are sinful. During our time of confession, we are encouraged to look within us to the ways that we, too are sinful. Let us approach God in prayer with contrite hearts—hearts of true repentance.

Prayer of Confession
LORD God, when we look around, we see all kinds of iniquity. Help us to look within. Help us to know when we have participated in the sin, we see all around. Help us to convict ourselves of the ways we have separated ourselves from your holiness. Help us to be repentant, and free us from our sins, that we may walk uprightly before you.

Assurance of Forgiveness
Our act of confession shows the faith that we have that, through Christ, our sins can be forgiven by a just, but gracious God. We will never be perfect, but through Jesus we can be redeemed. Thanks be to God for this promise of wholeness.

Offertory Invitation
What we have never seems to be enough. Yet, with the blessings of God through our Lord Jesus, even a few fish and loaves of bread were sufficient to feed many thousands. We are called to give all we can, so that, through the blessing of God, it may bring daily bread to many. Let us give as we are able.

Offertory Prayer
Take these gifts, O LORD. Add your blessings to them. Make them abundant beyond our ability to imagine or understand. Give us hearts and minds and spirits that are able to use all you have entrusted to us individually and as a community to serve you faithfully. Bless us as we give and bless our gifts. Amen.

Benediction
We have worshiped, and we have met with our God,
The Creator, the Savior, and the Holy Spirit,
The Three-in-one.
How can we leave unchanged?
Go now, with the blessings of God,
offering Christ's love to all you meet.
Amen.

Proper 14

Scripture
Genesis 37:1-4, 12-28 *or 1 Kings 19:9-18*
Psalm 105:1-6, 16-22 *or Psalm 85:8-13*
Romans 10:5-15
Matthew 14:22-33

Call to Worship
One: O give thanks to the LORD!
Call on God's name and make God's deeds known among the peoples.
Many: Sing to God! Sing praises to the LORD.
Tell of God's wonderful works!
One: Glory in the name of the LORD our God.
Let the hearts of those who seek the LORD rejoice!
Many: Seek the LORD and God's strength;
Seek God's presence continually.
One: Remember the wonderful works God has done.
Remember God's miracles, and the judgments God has uttered.
Many: O offspring of God's servant Abraham,
Children of Jacob, God's chosen ones, praise the LORD!

Invocation
LORD, you are our great redeemer and our powerful defender. Our sole purpose here this day is to worship you. Call us into worship. Open our hearts to hear your message in whatever way you choose to speak. Open our eyes to see you in this sanctuary and in each other. Open all our senses to experience you as fully as we possibly can. Amen.

Call to Confession
We who belong to Christ recognize that we are imperfect people. We will never reach the level of perfection for which we are called to strive. Instead, we remind ourselves to come this day and every time we gather in confession, asking for God's forgiveness for our missteps and trusting in the grace Christ offers. Let us pray.

Prayer of Confession
God of all grace, without your mercy, we would have no hope of salvation. But we know that you are a merciful and loving God, extending mercy to your people that can cover all our sins. We are heartily sorry for our misdeeds. It pains us to bring them to mind. Forgive us and make us whole once again.

Assurance of Forgiveness
Paul writes that if we confess with our lips that Jesus is Lord and believe in our hearts that God raised Christ from the dead, we will be saved. For one believes with the heart and is so justified. We have confessed our sins and have confessed faith in Christ by proclaiming Christ able to forgive all our sins. And as we have confessed, we have been completely forgiven. Thanks be to God!

Offertory Invitation
We often approach the time of offering as people of little faith, fearful to give. We are worried about ourselves, worried about our tomorrows. God calls us to give freely, that the world may share in the blessings we have received. Let us give all we can to the glory of God.

Offertory Prayer
Our treasures are here before you, O God. In this moment of prayer, accept our hearts and lives, too. Help us not only to give to you, help us to live to you, that we may be the shining stars you have called us to be in your world. Let us show your love to all people. Amen.

Benediction
How beautiful are the feet of those that bring the good news!
Go now, with the blessings of our LORD, the God of all the universe,
and carry the good news to all places where you may go!
Amen.

Proper 15

Scripture
Genesis 45:1-15 *or Isaiah 56:1, 6-8*
Psalm 133 *or Psalm 67*
Romans 11:1-2a, 29-32
Matthew 15: (10-20), 21-28

Call to Worship
One: May God be gracious to us and bless us!
May God's face shine upon us!
Many: Let the peoples praise you, O God;
Let all the peoples praise you.
One: Let God's way be known upon the earth, God's saving power among all nations.
Let nations be glad and sing for joy, for God judges with equity and guides all.
Many: Let the peoples praise you, O God;
Let all the peoples praise you.
One: The earth has yielded its increase; God, our God, has blessed us.
May God continue to bless us; let all the ends of the earth revere our God!
Many: Let the peoples praise you, O God;
Let all the peoples praise you!

Invocation
God, you and you alone are holy. You and you alone are worthy of praise. You and you alone are our God, mighty in power and awesome in strength! Send your Spirit among us this day. Refresh us, renew us, strengthen us. Re-make us in your image and make us to shine your light to all we may ever meet.
Amen.

Call to Confession
Paul writes that God has imprisoned all in sinfulness. All people on the earth are sinful creatures. We have strayed from God. We have followed our own paths. We have sought after the things that do not satisfy. Let us confess before God that we may be healed once again.

Prayer of Confession
Holy and loving God, you have seen our lack of faithfulness. Help us to call it to our own minds this day. We are sorry for ways we have neglected your calling in our lives. As individuals and as societies, we have chosen the easy way over the right way. We have forgotten to love one another. We have forgotten to place you first in our lives. Forgive us, we pray.

Assurance of Forgiveness
Paul also writes that people were imprisoned so that God may be merciful to all. When we come to God, confessing our sins and asking for forgiveness, God is quick to show mercy and relieve us of our burden. When we confess, we are forgiven. What a wonderful God we serve!

Offertory Invitation
Jesus reminds us in today's gospel reading that the things that show our true character, the things that defile, are the things that come out of our mouths and hearts. The gifts we give or withhold display our faithfulness. Let us give faithfully and generously, showing our love for God and God's people.

Offertory Prayer
LORD God shower your blessings on this offering. In your hands the gifts we have received here can become more than they could ever be on their own. We place these gifts and all our gifts into your hands that you may use our offerings and use us to bring your light to the world. Amen.

Benediction
Receive now blessings;
Blessings of our great Creator,
Blessings of our merciful Savior,
and blessings of the empowering Spirit,
That you may be strengthened for your journey.
Amen.

Proper 16

Scripture
Exodus 1:8-2:10 *or Isaiah 51:1-6*
Psalm 124 *or Psalm 138*
Romans 12:1-8
Matthew 16:13-20

Call to Worship
One: The LORD God is our helper and our strength.
God is the keeper of our souls.
Many: We shall not be put to shame,
For the great strength of the LORD is our shield.
One: If the LORD had not been on our side,
If it had not been the LORD who had protected us,
Many: We would have been swallowed up by our enemies.
In God's mercy, we have been rescued from their hands.
One: Our help is in the name of the LORD,
The LORD God, who made the heavens and the earth.
Many: We shall praise God's name forever!
Let all creation praise the name of the LORD!

Invocation
LORD, you are great indeed! When we read your word we see how you have provided for your people in unexpected and powerful ways. Send us your Spirit in new and unexpected ways this day. Let it flow around us and among us and within us, making us entirely yours. Change us, that we may better resemble our great example, Christ our Lord. Amen.

Call to Confession
We are called to a time of confession, because, recognizing our brokenness, we know that we are in need of healing. God offers that healing to all who will confess and repent of their sins. Because we believe in God's promises, we turn to God in this time of confession.

Prayer of Confession
Merciful God, we confess that we have strayed from your will for

our lives. Knowingly or unknowingly, we have been unfaithful to our promises. We have been unfaithful to you. Forgive our sins that we may be redeemed and help us to live lives worthy of your calling on us. Amen.

Assurance of Forgiveness
In amazing ways God has shown mercy to God's people. When the people were bound in slavery, God sent Moses as deliverer. When people were bound in sinfulness, God sent a deliverer in Jesus the Christ. Through Jesus' love and mercy, we have been redeemed, and we are forgiven. Thanks be to God!

Offertory Invitation
Nothing but our best will do. As we approach this time of offering, let us examine ourselves. What are we willing to give to God? What are we holding back? Let us give all we can, so that the world can be healed through the love and grace of our Lord, Jesus the Christ.

Offertory Prayer
Holy One, please accept these gifts which we offer to you this day and bless them. Bless them that they may be food for the hungry, clothing for the unclothed, water to the thirsty, and good news to many. Help us to wisely use all our gifts that they may better glorify you. Amen.

Benediction
Let us go now,
Presenting our bodies as living sacrifices,
Holy and acceptable to God,
Through the Messiah, Jesus the Christ.
And may God's blessing go with each of us,
as we go to do God's work in the world. Amen.

Proper 17

Scripture
Exodus 3:1-15 *or Jeremiah 15:15-21*
Psalm 105:1-6, 23-26, 45b *or Psalm 26:1-8*
Romans 12:9-21
Matthew 16:21-28

Call to Worship
One: O give thanks to the LORD, call on God's name!
Make known God's deeds among all the peoples.
Many: Sing to God, sing praises! Tell of God's wonderful works.
Glory in God's holy name.
One: Let the hearts of all who seek the LORD rejoice!
Seek the LORD's strength; seek God's presence continually.
Many: Remember the wonderful works God has done.
Remember the LORD's miracles and judgments.
One: Remember these things, for we are God's people.
We have been called to follow the LORD in all our days.
Many: Give great thanks to the LORD;
Give praises and thanks unto God!

Invocation
Holy God, you have called us aside to see your wonderful works. You have called us from the lives that we are living and asked us to serve you in sometimes frightening ways. We, like Moses, have sometimes been reluctant. Strengthen us with your Spirit. Give us the courage to face the trials we have ahead so we can serve you in truth. Amen.

Call to Confession
The call to bless those who persecute us and to live in harmony with all others is sometimes hard for us to follow. We know we have not followed God's commands perfectly. When we have cursed another or when we have spread discord we have sinned. Let us confess.

Prayer of Confession
Ever-living and loving God, we confess that we have not blessed

those who persecute us. We have not always blessed those who have blessed us. We have not lived in harmony with your creation, but have instead valued ourselves more highly than others, giving in to envy, jealousy, and deceit. Forgive us, we pray, and help us to be the people you have called us to be.

Assurance of Forgiveness
The good news of the gospel is that Jesus' Christ's life, death, and resurrection give salvation to those who believe in him. When we humbly ask for forgiveness in Christ's name, we are made clean every time. All the things you have confessed have been washed away through the grace of Christ. Rejoice, faithful ones of God!

Offertory Invitation
Paul exhorts us to contribute to the needs of the saints and extend hospitality to strangers. Our offering is one way that we can begin to do this. Let us enter into the time of offering prayerfully, giving of what we have and what we are to God's work and glory.

Offertory Prayer
Loving God, together our offerings are much more than they could ever be individually. When blessed by you, they can do what to us is unimaginable. Take these gifts and use them to your glory. Help us to have the wisdom to use what you have given us to care for others and to give your love. We ask this in Jesus' name.
Amen.

Benediction
Go with the blessings of God,
The Creator,
The Savior,
And the Holy Spirit,
And do not be overcome by evil,
But overcome evil with good.
Amen.

Proper 18

Scripture
Exodus 12:1-14 *or Ezekiel 33:7-11*
Psalm 149 *or Psalm 119:33-40*
Romans 13:8-14
Matthew 18:15-20

Call to Worship
One: Praise the LORD! Sing to the LORD a new song!
Sing God's praise in the assembly of the faithful.
Many: Let Israel be glad in its Maker,
Let the children of God rejoice in their Ruler!
One: Let them praise God's name with dancing,
Making melody to God with tambourine and lyre.
Many: Let the faithful exult in glory,
Let them sing to God for joy.
One: Let the high praises of God be in their throats,
And the worship of God be in their souls.
Many: Let them glory in the LORD their God,
The Maker and Redeemer of all!

Invocation
We worship you, Mighty God, with all we have, all we are, and all we hope to be. Visit us in this place today. Shower your blessings on us. Breathe into our hearts and minds, filling us with your wonder, with your Spirit. Be in this place with us, move in us, re-invigorate us to give you all we are. Amen.

Call to Confession
Love does no wrong to a neighbor, therefore love is the fulfillment of the law. Paul wrote these words to help the Roman church and all of us know how to live blamelessly. But we have loved imperfectly, and this has allowed us to be sinful, breaking God's laws. Let us confess before our God.

Prayer of Confession
LORD, you have called us to love, but we have not loved as you called. We have hurt one another in greed, in desire for things that

do not satisfy, in our lack of ability to love as you love. Forgive us. Forgive our lack of love, and heal us, not only so we may be forgiven, but so we can set aside the things that keep us from loving others as we love ourselves.

Assurance of Forgiveness
The Lord Jesus has come that we might have life and have it abundantly. Christ's gift to us is the gift of salvation, allowing us to be forgiven even when we have sinned. We have come as a body of Christ, in order to confess our sins. When we confess we are forgiven. Christ won the victory and allows us to be victors also!

Offertory Invitation
Our love for God through Christ compels us to do good things for one another. It also causes our hearts to be filled with compassion for all those the world over who live in need and want. We believe God desires abundant life for all. Our gifts in the time of offering are one way to provide for those in need. Let us give generously, as we have been blessed generously.

Offertory Prayer
You have blessed us indeed, O LORD, and out of those blessings we have brought these gifts to you. We pray that you would take and use them. Make them grow with your blessing. Give life to the world through what we have brought here and through our other gifts of time and talent, offered to you. Amen.

Benediction
Owe nothing to anyone,
Except to love one another.
And may the God of love bless you richly,
as you follow the commandment of love in your life.
Amen.

Proper 19

Scripture
Exodus 14:19-31 *or Exodus 15:1b-11, 20-21, or Genesis 50:15-21*
Psalm 114 *or Psalm 103:(1-7), 8-13*
Romans 14:1-12
Matthew 18:21-35

Call to Worship
One: Bless the LORD, O my soul, and all that is within me.
Bless God's holy name, and do not forget all God's benefits.
Many: God forgives iniquity and heals diseases.
God redeems life from the Pit and crowns the faithful with steadfast love and mercy.
One: God satisfies with good as long as life endures.
The LORD renews the youth of the faithful, making them like eagles.
Many: The LORD works vindication and justice for all who are oppressed.
God is merciful and gracious, slow to anger and abounding in steadfast love.
One: The LORD does not always accuse, nor will God keep anger forever.
God does not deal with us according to our sins, nor repay us for iniquity.
Many: As far as the east is from the west, are our sins removed from us.
Like a parent has compassion for children, so the LORD has compassion for God's children.

Invocation
You care for us, Gracious God, like a parent cares for a child. We are your children, and we need you for our daily sustenance, our continuing guidance, and our spiritual existence. Allow your Spirit to flow into us and through us this day. Let us meet you here, and let our minds, bodies, and spirits be changed by encountering you. Amen.

Call to Confession
We will all be accountable to God for our own actions. God has offered us the opportunity to be cleansed from our sins by turning to God and offering our sincere repentance for those sins. Let us pray to God that we may be healed.

Prayer of Confession
Loving God, we confess that we have sinned against you and against your people. We have missed the mark you have set for us, and often we have done so without much thought for your desires for us. Please make us completely repentant and grant us forgiveness that we may be whole in your sight.

Assurance of Forgiveness
The grace of our Lord, Jesus Christ, surpasses all our understanding. We are fortunate to be able to come before our Lord, asking for forgiveness, and knowing that through Christ's grace, that forgiveness is available to all who repent. Beloved of God, you are forgiven.

Offertory Invitation
Sometimes living into the kingdom of God seems to cost us more than we can afford. Yet there is nothing that is worth more than what we have received from God. In these moments, let us return some of our blessings to God to glorify God and to care for God's people.

Offertory Prayer
You have blessed us, and we have willingly received. Now, LORD, receive from us gifts that are intended for your glory in the world. Let them be used to benefit your people, wherever they are found, that all people may live the type of abundant life you desire for us. Amen.

Benediction
We do not live to ourselves, and we do not die to ourselves.
If we live, we live to the Lord,
and if we die, we die to the Lord,
So that, whether we live, or we die, we are the Lord's.
Go with God's blessing, To live for and serve our Lord, Jesus the Christ. Amen.

Proper 20

Scripture
Exodus 16:2-15 *or Jonah 3:10-4:11*
Psalm 105:1-6, 37-45 *or Psalm 145:1-8*
Philippians 1:21-30
Matthew 20:1-16

Call to Worship
One: O give thanks to the LORD, call on God's name,
Make known the deeds of our God among all the peoples.
Many: Sing to God, sing great praises unto the LORD.
Tell of all God's wonderful works!
One: Glory in the holy name of the LORD.
Let the hearts of those who seek God rejoice.
Many: Remember the wonderful works that God has done.
Remember God's miracles and all judgments.
One: For God brought food to the Israelites in the desert places.
God brought forth life sustaining water from the rock.
Many: The LORD has remembered the covenant with Abraham
and sustained the people!
Sing praises to the LORD, our God!

Invocation
You have invited us into this holy space today, LORD of the universe, to meet with you. We are in awe of you, and we long for you to make yourself known in this place. Speak clearly to us here. Show images of who you are. Make us to recognize you in our time of worship, and fill our spiritual hunger with your love, your sustenance, and your refreshing and cleansing waters. Amen.

Call to Confession
We are often like Jonah, quick to judge others. He was even willing to disobey God so others would not receive forgiveness. Let us confess to God ways that we have disobeyed in order that our own wants or needs may be fulfilled instead of the purposes God has given to us.

Prayer of Confession
LORD, we are humbled by your grace. We confess that we have often looked to our own desires instead of the needs of your people. We have valued ourselves more highly than others and neglected your call to love others as ourselves. Forgive us, we pray, and plant love within our hearts that we may fulfill your calling to us as followers of you and your Son, Jesus the Christ.

Assurance of Forgiveness
God has called us to this time of confession, because God desires to forgive the people. God wants us to repent so that God may give us the salvation we so desperately want and so clearly do not deserve. Because we have confessed and because we have repented, God is willing to forgive. Thanks be to God!

Offertory Invitation
The gifts we have, we have received from the vast storehouses of God. We are only able to share those gifts with others for the short time that we are on the earth. Let us make the most of that time by giving to others so that all humanity may know the love of the God we serve.

Offertory Prayer
We lay our treasures before you, Holy One, and we offer them to you completely. Please give your blessing to these gifts that they may become more than simply treasures, but that they may show your love to all creation. May we dedicate all we are to this purpose. Amen.

Benediction
Beloved, as you leave this place
live your lives in a manner worthy of the gospel of Christ.
Share Christ's love with all you meet.
In this way God will be glorified, and the world will be blessed.
Amen.

Proper 21

Scripture
Exodus 17:1-7 *or Ezekiel 18:1-4, 25-32*
Psalm 78:1-4, 12-16 *or Psalm 25:1-9*
Philippians 2:1-13
Matthew 21:23-32

Call to Worship
One: Give ear, O people, to the teaching of our God.
Incline your ears to the words of our LORD.
Many: God speaks to the people in parables, dark sayings from of old.
Things we have heard and known, that our ancestors have told us.
One: We will tell them to the coming generations.
We will tell our children of the glorious deeds of the LORD, God's might, and wonders.
Many: In the sight of our ancestors God worked marvels in the land of Egypt.
God divided the sea and let them pass through it, making the waters stand like a heap.
One: In the daytime, God led the people with a cloud.
All night long, the LORD led the people with a fiery light.
Many: God split rocks in the wilderness and made streams flow from the rocks.
God gave them to drink abundantly and caused waters to flow down like rivers.

Invocation
In the days that the Israelites were in the wilderness, LORD of all, you filled them with water and nourished them with food. Even in the midst of the desert, you restored your people. Restore us this day. Send your Spirit to quench our thirst and to satisfy our hunger. Renew us in your love for this day and for every day, that we may serve you fully. Amen.

Call to Confession
Humility is a strong theme in our Holy **Scripture**. We are admonished time and again to humble ourselves before God, not

thinking of ourselves more highly than we ought. This time of confession is a time for deep humility as we seek to be granted forgiveness for our misdeeds. Let us confess together.

Prayer of Confession
Holy and awesome God, we bow before you now, humbly confessing our many sins. We have not loved you in the way you have taught. We have not loved each other as we should. In our thoughts, our words, and our actions we have betrayed our own sense of entitlement. Forgive us, we pray, and lead us in your everlasting truth.

Assurance of Forgiveness
God is at work in the people of God. When we are willing to confess, when we are willing to repent, and when we come before God, praying for the strength to turn from our sinful ways, God will forgive. God will strengthen us to be better people. God will give us the redemption for which we so desperately long. Thanks to God for this awesome act of grace.

Offertory Invitation
What shall we give to God, rich or poor, young or old? We all have the same gift to give. It is the gift of true devotion. When we give this gift, we will not count the cost of what we dedicate to God, we will simply give out of love and in joy for the coming kingdom. Let us give our devotion first, then our offerings.

Offertory Prayer
Holy and Ancient One, we offer ourselves to you in these moments of praise. Please accept our offerings to you, offerings of our gifts of money, our gifts of time, and our gifts of service. Help us to use all we can to glorify you. Amen.

Benediction
May the grace of God, a grace which passes all understanding,
The overwhelming love of our Savior, Jesus the Christ,
And the empowering flame of the Holy Spirit
Be with you all, now and forever more.
Amen.

Proper 22

Scripture
Exodus 20:1-4, 7-9, 12-20 *or Isaiah 5:1-7*
Psalm 19 *or Psalm 80:7-15*
Philippians 3:4b-14
Matthew 21:33-46

Call to Worship
One: God spoke all these words, "I am the LORD your God,
You shall have no other gods before me.
Many: You shall not make for yourself an idol,
You shall not misuse the name of the LORD your God.
One: Remember the Sabbath and keep it holy,
Honor your father and your mother.
Many: You shall not murder.
You shall not commit adultery.
One: You shall not steal.
You shall not bear false witness against your neighbor.
Many: You shall not covet anything that belongs to your neighbor."
God desires that the people do what is right.

Invocation
We revere you, Awesome God, and we thank you for your laws given to us. You have taught us to be your servants and you have taught us how to live your ways. Move in us now that these decrees would not solely be in our minds, but that they would be written directly on our hearts. Help us to follow you in love, and not in fear. Amen.

Call to Confession
As Paul writes, even those who may feel that they have the most boasting to do in their adherence to God's law are still sinners in need of redemption. We enter this time of confession so that we may be forgiven of the sins we have committed and so that we may truly repent before our God. Let us confess together.

Prayer of Confession
Maker of all, we confess that we have been incapable of keeping your commands to us. We have thought of ourselves and we have chased after things that we felt would satisfy us rather than following after you and practicing your love to people. Forgive us. Heal us. Renew us, that we may follow you alone.

Assurance of Forgiveness
Our righteousness comes not through any deeds we may have committed or avoided, but through the faith that we have in Christ Jesus. Through our faith in Christ, even when we have been unable to follow God properly, God will forgive our sins and make us as if we were truly righteous. Thanks be to God!

Offertory Invitation
The gifts we give and that the church receives in this time of offering are dedicated solely to the purposes of God in this world. We have an obligation and a privilege to care for one another and to support the witness of Christ in the world. Let us give as we are able to these causes.

Offertory Prayer
God of All, we thank you that you have given us so many gifts. We return these gifts to you this day. Bless them, watch over them, multiply them that they may be blessings for you and for your kingdom on earth. We pray these things in the name of Christ our Savior, Amen.

Benediction
As we leave this place,
Let us go, pressing on toward the goal for the prize of the heavenly call in Christ Jesus,
And may the Great Three-In-One God
Bless us all as we strive to serve.
Amen.

Proper 23

Scripture
Exodus 32:1-14 *or Isaiah 25:1-9*
Psalm 106:1-6, 19-23 *or Psalm 23*
Philippians 4:1-9
Matthew 22:1-14

Call to Worship
One: Praise the LORD! O give thanks to the LORD, for God is good.
God's steadfast love endures forever!
Many: Who can utter the mighty doings of God?
Who can declare the praise of the LORD?
One: Happy are those who observe justice,
Happy are those who do righteousness at all times.
Many: Remember us, O LORD, when you show favor to your people.
Help us as you deliver those who belong to you.
One: Allow us, O LORD, to see the prosperity of your chosen ones.
Let us rejoice in the gladness of your world, that we may glory in your heritage.
Many: We praise you for your grace and mercy on our behalf.
May the praise of the LORD be ever on our lips and God's love ever in our hearts!

Invocation
LORD God, Almighty One of the universe, your steadfast love endures from generation to generation, protecting us, healing us, and empowering us to do your work. As we gather in worship this day we seek to know you, to hear from you, and to express our love for you. Fill this place with your presence, help us to recognize you, and make us ever newly devoted to your praise. Amen.

Call to Confession
In all generations, people have sinned. The people who had just been led out of bondage from Egypt sinned when Moses was

away too long. They had just seen God's power made manifest in the world, and they faltered so quickly. Are modern worshipers any different? Let us confess.

Prayer of Confession
LORD of all, great Master of all things, and God of grace, we confess that we, like our ancestors, have placed other things in front of you in our lives. Sometimes this has been ourselves. Sometimes it has been the pursuit of wealth or power or some other worldly thing. Please forgive us. Help us to clearly see our errors and lead us to follow you in truth and faithfulness.

Assurance of Forgiveness
Even in Moses' day, God spared the people from their sins. In our day, we have an advocate, Jesus the Christ, who intercedes on our behalf. We are blessed to receive forgiveness from a loving God when we confess and turn from our sin. People of God, you are forgiven.

Offertory Invitation
The gifts we have received and that we enjoy are not for our benefit alone. We are called, as followers of Christ, to give of what we have received for the rest of the world to know the love of God, and abundance of life. Let us give generously that God's work may be done.

Offertory Prayer
God of all good gifts bless these gifts we have brought to you. We pray that these gifts may be acceptable to you and that they may serve your purposes in your world. May our will be so aligned with yours that whatever you desire for these gifts we may gladly do. Amen.

Benediction
Do not worry about anything,
But in everything by prayer and supplication with thanksgiving
Let your requests be made known to God.
And the peace of God,
Which passes all understanding,
Guard your hearts and minds in Christ Jesus. Amen

Proper 24

Scripture
Exodus 33:12-23 *or Isaiah 45:1-7*
Psalm 99 *or Psalm 96:1-9, (10-13)*
1 Thessalonians 1:1-10
Matthew 22:15-22

Call to Worship
One: The LORD is ruler over all; let the peoples tremble!
God sits enthroned upon the cherubim; let the earth quake!
Many: The LORD is great in all the earth, God is exalted over the peoples.
Let them praise your great and awesome name! Holy is God!
One: Mighty ruler, lover of justice, you have established equity.
You have executed justice and righteousness in the people.
Many: Extol the LORD our God!
Worship at God's holy footstool. Holy is God!
One: LORD, you answered the cry of our ancestors,
You are a forgiving and loving God to all generations.
Many: Extol the LORD our God, and worship at God's holy mountain.
For the LORD our God is holy!

Invocation
Like Moses, O God, we often dream of seeing you in all your glory. But like all people, we know we cannot experience your full glory. Give us a glimpse of yourself today. Help us to recognize you in our worship, in our music, in our silences, in your word proclaimed, and in one another. Make us to know you better in this place. Amen.

Call to Confession
Our sins are ever before us. We may wish it were not so, but there is nothing we can keep from God. God knows our every outward and inward way. Let us confess to God the ways we know we have been unfaithful, let us pray to God to enlighten us to ways we do not even recognize, and let us ask for God's forgiveness.

Prayer of Confession
Great and Gracious God, we confess that we have sinned against you and against your creation. We bring to mind our sins today, the ones we recognize, and we pray for wisdom to discern other ways that we have veered from your path. Forgive us. Make us whole. Grant that we may truly repent and be better servants of you.

Assurance of Forgiveness
The great gift of Christ is the gift of salvation. We, who have come to God, confessing Christ and asking for forgiveness of our sins, have been forgiven through the gifts Christ gave to the world. May the grace of Christ surround us all in this day and evermore.

Offertory Invitation
Jesus said to give to Caesar what belonged to Caesar and give to God what belonged to God. We profess that all things belong to God, so we should hold nothing back from our giving to God. Let us worship God with the giving of all our gifts, our treasures, our time, and our talents, to God's glory.

Offertory Prayer
Thank you, God, for blessing us with so many wonderful gifts. We praise you for all the things you have given, our lives, our abilities, our possessions. Help us to dedicate them all to your work in the world. Bless these gifts that they may bring your love to your people wherever they are found. Amen.

Benediction
Go now,
As imitators of the Lord,
Showing Christ's love and mercy to all you meet.
And may God's blessings go with you as you seek to do God's will.
Amen.

Proper 25

Scripture
Deuteronomy 34:1-12 *or Leviticus 19:1-2, 15-18*
Psalm 90:1-6, 13-17 *or Psalm 1*
1 Thessalonians 2:1-8
Matthew 22:34-46

Call to Worship
One: O LORD, you have been our dwelling place in all generations.
Before the mountains were brought forth, or ever you had formed creation,
Many: From everlasting to everlasting you are God.
For a thousand years in your sight are like yesterday when it is past.
One: You turn us back to dust, and say, "Turn back, you mortals."
Our days are like a dream, like grass that is renewed in the morning.
Many: In the morning it flourishes and is renewed.
In the evening it fades and withers.
One: Let your work be manifest to your servants,
And your glorious power to their children.
Many: Let your favor be upon us, LORD our God,
And prosper us for the work of our hands.

Invocation
Holy and everlasting God, we enter your sanctuary in awe. We have come to meet with you, the very God of the entire cosmos. We may wonder who we are to meet with you, yet you have called us into relationship with yourself. Give eyes to see, ears to hear your presence, your majesty, your Spirit. Make us to know you, to worship you, and to give ourselves to you alone. Amen.

Call to Confession
From earliest days the hearts of humans have been bent to sinfulness. The very make-up of our human selves seems to work against us, keeping us from being the people we want to be. In this time of worship, we lift to God our confessions and ask that God forgive us and make us clean. Let us confess together.

Prayer of Confession
LORD God, you are all holiness and all perfection. Because of your perfection, we are sometimes afraid to even approach you with our confessions. We have failed in many ways to be who we know you have called us to be. You commanded us to love, but we choose to separate from you and others. Forgive us and show us your way once more.

Assurance of Forgiveness
The very Son of God is willing to intercede for humanity, offering blessing and offering the opportunity for forgiveness, even when we have erred badly. This grace, offered by God through the Christ, and with the guidance of the Holy Spirit is ours when we ask and repent. People of God, we are forgiven this day! Thanks be to God!

Offertory Invitation
The work of God is of the heavenly realm, but it is to be performed in our world. One reality of our world is a need for monetary resources to do the work to which God has called us as individuals and the church as a community. Let us give generously that our work may be pleasing to God.

Offertory Prayer
Holy Author of Life, we pray that these gifts are acceptable to you. We offer them to you completely. Take them, bless them, and use them for the uplifting of your kingdom everywhere creation exists. We pray this in the name of your Son, Jesus the Christ. Amen.

Benediction
As we leave this place,
Let us go,
Sharing the gospel,
And sharing of ourselves with those we meet.
And may God our great Creator, Savior, and Guide
Bless you all,
Until we meet again. Amen.

Proper 26

Scripture
Joshua 3:7-17 *or Micah 3:5-12*
Psalm 107:1-7, 33-37 *or Psalm 43*
1 Thessalonians 2:9-13
Matthew 23:1-12

Call to Worship
One: O give thanks to the LORD, for God is good!
The LORD's steadfast love endures forever!
Many: Let the redeemed of the LORD say so, those God redeemed from trouble.
And gathered in from the lands, from the east and the west, from the north and the south.
One: Let us thank the LORD for God's steadfast love,
Thanks be for God's wonderful works to humankind!
Many: For God satisfies the thirsty, and the hungry God fills with good things.
God turns deserts into pools of water, a parched land into springs of water.
One: God establishes places within the parched lands,
Places for the hungry to live and be satisfied.
Many: In those places they will eat their fill.
They will sow fields and plant vineyards and receive a fruitful yield.

Invocation
Glory to you, O God of all the universe! We have come here to proclaim your wonders. We have come here to witness your healing. We have come here to learn about and grow in you. We rejoice that you have come to meet us in this place! Fill us with your presence and renew your Spirit within us, that we may ever become more like you. Amen.

Call to Confession
God calls us to ask for forgiveness of our sins and to repent. God gives us the promise that when we truly search our hearts, truly humble ourselves, and truly work to live righteously, God will

forgive us of our sins and remove them from us. Let us pray that we may be cleansed.

Prayer of Confession
Holy One, you indeed are the only one who is to be called holy. We confess that we have not lived in your holy way. We have traded our love of you for love of idols. We have traded our love of one another for our own greedy purposes. Forgive us, we pray. Cleanse our hearts that we may not be drawn to sin and help us to live our lives in the way you have taught.

Assurance of Forgiveness
The grace of the Lord Jesus the Christ be with you! When we have come to God, confessing our sins, and when we have asked God for forgiveness, determining to live in God's way, God will be faithful, through the grace of Christ, to forgive. As you have confessed, you are forgiven! Praise be to God!

Offertory Invitation
The gifts God has given to us and all creation are more than we could ever begin to count. It is our privilege to give back to God a portion of the gifts we have received. Let us offer our sacrifices now to God as a heartfelt act of worship.

Offertory Prayer
Creator of all, we ask that you would receive the gifts, given by your people who love you and who wish to serve you. Bless these gifts and their givers that not only may the treasures we have collected this day be dedicated to you, but also our very hearts, minds, and bodies. We pray that your kingdom would be manifest here on earth, and we give to offer life to all. Amen

Benediction
May the grace of the Lord, Jesus the Christ,
The overwhelming love of God,
And the communion of God's Holy Spirit
Be with all of us as we leave this place,
And forever more.
Amen.

Proper 27

Scripture
Joshua 24:1-3a, 14-25 *or Amos 5:18-24*
Psalm 78:1-7 *or Psalm 70*
1 Thessalonians 4:13-18
Matthew 25:1-13

Call to Worship
One: Give ear, O people, to the teaching of the word.
Incline your ears to the words of the psalmist.
Many: The writer speaks to us in a parable,
Uttering dark sayings from of old.
One: Things that we have both known and heard,
Things that our ancestors have taught us.
Many: We will not hide them from our children;
We will tell the coming generations of the glorious deeds of the LORD.
One: We will relate to them God's might, and the wonders God has done,
For God commanded our ancestors of old to teach God's decrees to their children.
Many: We teach, so that the coming generations might know our God,
That they may have their hope in the LORD and never forget God's works.

Invocation
We choose this day to serve you, and you alone, Holy God of the Universe! We come to be with you, to experience your presence, and to show you the reverence and love that you deserve. We come to learn of you, that your presence may fill us up and cause us to abandon our unholy wants and desires. Make us holy as you are holy, O God, in this time of worship. Amen.

Call to Confession
The prophet Amos writes about human efforts for atonement. Even the commanded sacrifices God proclaimed to be unworthy through Amos and other prophets. What God desires is

humbleness of heart, return to God as sole ruler of our hearts, and truthful repentance. Let us offer our confessions to God.

Prayer of Confession
Gracious One, we confess that we have tried to live our lives honoring both your world and our world. We revere you, but we continue to value the things of this world. We are sorry for the pain this has caused to your children, to you, and to us. Please forgive us, and help us to choose to serve only you.

Assurance of Forgiveness
Christ's love for us provided our source of forgiveness. Even though all humans are sinful, and even though we are unable to make atonement for ourselves, God has made a way through our savior for our sins to be washed away. When we confess and truly repent, we can be made whole. In the name of Christ Jesus, we have been forgiven.

Offertory Invitation
What shall we give to God for all the blessings God has given to us? It is impossible to repay. Instead, during this time of worship, we offer our tithes, our offerings, and our dedication to God and to God's work in the world. Let us worship God with these gifts.

Offertory Prayer
LORD, you have heard our prayers for forgiveness this day, and you have now received our offerings, given in gratitude to you. We pray for your blessings on all these offerings. Please increase them in their value and in their effectiveness to serve you and your people in this world. We dedicate our lives to you. Amen.

Benediction
Our hope is nothing less than an eternity spent with one another and with God.
May God bless us so that we may attain this goal,
And may we bless others with the good news that can help them to attain the goal also.
May it be so.
Amen.

Proper 28

Scripture
Judges 4:1-7 *or Zephaniah 1:7, 12-18*
Psalm 123 *or Psalm 90:1-8, (9-11), 12*
1 Thessalonians 5:1-11
Matthew 25:14-30

Call to Worship
One: To you we lift up our eyes, O God!
To you, who are enthroned in the heavens.
Many: As the servant looks to the master, or the maid to her mistress,
So, our eyes look to the LORD our God, until God has mercy on us.
One: Have mercy upon us, O God.
Have mercy upon your people.
Many: For you, O LORD, have been our dwelling place in all generations.
From everlasting to everlasting, you are God.
One: Before the mountains were brought forth,
And before you had formed the earth and the world,
Many: You were enthroned in majesty even then.
For all generations and for time inconceivable, you are our God!

Invocation
LORD God, you are the God of all time and spaces, the God outside our understanding of time and outside the universe that we know. You are powerful beyond measure, amazing beyond our capacity to dream, and wonderful beyond our best thoughts. Teach us of you. Let us learn of your ways. Let us see you clearly, let us hear your voice in our time of worship, and let us become new creations in this time with you. Amen.

Call to Confession
Even when we try to be perfect in God's eyes, we cannot do so. And often we do not even try as we should. It is clear that we have missed the mark in God's eyes and in our attempts to be God's people. We have much to confess. Let us confess together before our God.

Prayer of Confession
Holy One, you are the only One who is truly holy. In our best of times we try to be the holy people you have commanded us to be. We stumble even then. In other times, we are so consumed with the things of this world we aren't even doing our best to follow. Help us to reorder our lives. Help us to live as you have asked us to live. Forgive us this day and renew our hearts once more.

Assurance of Forgiveness
God does not desire wrath for us. Instead, God desires for us to obtain salvation through the Lord Jesus the Christ. God has asked us to humble ourselves and confess our sins before God, that we might be forgiven. When we do this, our faithful God will forgive. We offer our thanks to the God of grace.

Offertory Invitation
It is our duty and a great opportunity to give during these moments of worship. We give our tithes and we give our gifts of all our possessions, and of our willingness to serve. May we be found faithful in our offering this day.

Offertory Prayer
God, you are generous and loving to us. When we look truthfully at all the blessings we have received, we are humbled to realize that you have given so much to us in love. We pray that these gifts we return to you may receive your blessing, so they may be shared with others who are in need. We pray that your will may be done through all our gifts. Amen.

Benediction
May the God who loves us all,
Care for you and remain always with you,
Until we meet again,
And may we encourage one another,
And build each other up,
To do God's work in this world.
Amen.

Proper 29 Reign of Christ

Scripture
Ezekiel 34:11-16, 20-24
Psalm 100 *or Psalm 95:1-7a*
Ephesians 1:15-23
Matthew 25:31-46

Call to Worship
One: Make a joyful noise to the LORD, all the earth!
Worship the LORD with gladness; come into God's presence with singing.
Many: Know that the LORD is God. It is the LORD alone who has made us.
We are God's people, and the sheep of God's pasture.
One: Enter God's gates with thanksgiving.
Enter the courts of the LORD with praise!
Many: Give thanks to the great God of all ages.
Bless the name of the LORD most high.
One: For the LORD, our God, is good.
God's steadfast love endures forever.
Many: God's love for creation indeed endures for all ages and times!
God's faithfulness extends through all generations.

Invocation
Ruler of All the universe, we come today to bow before you and to offer our praise to you. We are awed by your majesty and we are grateful for your love. As we reach toward you in this time, allow us to experience your presence in new and powerful ways. Enlighten our eyes to see you. Enlighten our minds to know you. Help us to learn of you and learn how better to be your people. This is our heartfelt prayer this day. Amen.

Call to Confession
We are called to be a light to the world and a lamp in the darkness. We are called to serve those who are in need and take up our crosses to follow Christ. Although our intentions may be good, we have often missed the mark God set for us to show love for all creation. We need to confess.

Prayer of Confession
Awesome and loving God, we confess that we have sinned against you. In ways we recognize, and likely in many ways we do not, we have not followed your path, not placed you above the things of the world, and not cared for our sisters and brothers as we should. Please forgive us. Please show us where we have gone astray, and please help us to be the people we should be.

Assurance of Forgiveness
The ruler of all has made a way for us through grace to be reconciled to God. God promises that when we confess our sins and humbly bow before God, working toward repentance, God will forgive us. Because we have humbled ourselves and because we have prayed earnestly to God this day, God has forgiven us. Thanks to the God of grace!

Offertory Invitation
Jesus' words convict us that when we see the needs of those around us, we are not to ignore them. Instead, we are to do what we can to relieve the suffering of others in need. One way we can work toward this is by giving to the needs of the church, that the church may be a blessing to the community. Let us give as we are able.

Offertory Prayer
Holy God, mighty and awesome LORD, we offer these gifts to you. We pray that you would bless these gifts of our money, and also the gifts we offer in our hearts of our time, our abilities, and our compassion for others. May we bless the wider world through these gifts, and may your name be glorified through them. Amen.

Benediction
May the God of our Lord Jesus Christ
Give you a spirit of wisdom and revelation
As you come to know God,
So that, with the eyes of your heart enlightened,
You may know the hope to which you have been called,
The riches of God's grace,
And the immeasurable greatness of God's power.
Amen.

All Saints Day

Scripture
Daniel 7:1-3, 15-18
Psalm 149
Ephesians 1:11-23
Luke 6:20-31

Call to Worship
One: Praise the LORD! Sing to the LORD a new song!
Sing God's praise in the assembly of the faithful!
Many: Let all the earth be glad in its maker.
Let the children of God rejoice in their King!
One: Let them praise God's name with dancing,
Making melody to God with tambourine and lyre.
Many: For the LORD takes pleasure in God's people.
God adorns the humble with victory.
One: Let the faithful exult in glory;
Let them sing aloud to God for joy.
Many: Let the high praises of God be in their throats.
Let them proclaim the glory of our God. Praise the LORD!

Invocation
We praise you God, because you are the eternal one. You call things into being out of nothing. You redeem your creation. We praise you for those who have walked your path before us, those who have run their race and fought the good fight. We pray for the goodness of all people everywhere and for the soon to come communion with you and all creation in the redeemed world. Amen.

Call to Confession
God calls us to a time of confession. It is a sacred opportunity to unburden ourselves of the things we have done that have separated us from obedience to God in our lives. Let us call to mind our sinful ways and let us offer our repentance before a gracious God.

Prayer of Confession
LORD, hear our prayer. We are your servants, but we have not served you in all goodness or with all our hearts. We have allowed other concerns to get in our way of devotion to you. We have not followed your rule to do unto others as we would have them do unto us. Forgive us, we pray.

Assurance of Forgiveness
God's power to redeem was made manifest in the resurrection of Christ our Lord. Through Christ's resurrection, the victory over death is complete. Through Christ's atonement, we can have the same victory over sin, when we are willing to confess. Redemption is ours in our Lord, Jesus Christ!

Offertory Invitation
The gifts of the saints throughout the years have brought us to this place. A great blessing for us is to be able to give to the church and to its ministries that we may sustain the worshiping community into new generations. Let us give, in love, that the world may know God's good news.

Offertory Prayer
Giving and loving God, we bring our sacrifices to you, offering them for your use and for the uplifting of your kingdom here on earth. We thank you for gifts that have sustained us in the past and we pray that all we offer here may be used to glorify you and to empower your Church for its work in the world. Amen.

Benediction
May the God of our Lord Jesus Christ give you a spirit of wisdom and revelation,
As you come to know God,
So that, with the eyes of your hearts enlightened,
You may know the hope to which God has called you,
The riches of God's glorious inheritance among the saints,
And the immeasurable greatness of God's power.
Amen.

www.ingramcontent.com/pod-product-compliance
Lightning Source LLC
Chambersburg PA
CBHW052148110526
44591CB00012B/1903